The Gospel and My Black Skin

The Black freedom struggle has been the leaven in the modern democratic loaf just as the prophetic Black church has been the engine of the Black freedom struggle. This courageous and visionary book keeps our great Black tradition of love and justice alive. I salute Dr. JP Foster. His powerful and poignant witness is so timely in our grim times.

—Dr. Cornel West, Dietrich Bonhoeffer Chair, Union Theological Seminary; author of more than twenty books

It is rare to find the pastor-scholar who when striking the iron transforms the anvil itself with force under heat. Dr. JP Foster combines a blazing intellect with a pastoral heart producing a timely, relevant, and robust curriculum for those of us with big questions about race and the gospel. Reading this work won't require you to sacrifice your ethnicity for right convictions about the gospel, neither will it compromise conviction for tribe. We need that. I wish every young person I know had this for required reading.

—Rev. Dr. Charlie Dates, Senior Pastor, Salem Baptist Church and Progressive Baptist Church in Chicago; author, *What Hath Justice to Do with Righteousness?*

For anyone who's ever felt like they had to leave their culture at the door to follow Jesus, *The Gospel and My Black Skin* is the wake-up call we've been waiting for. Dr. JP Foster gets real about the Slave Bible, a version of faith that was literally cut to pieces to hide the God of the exodus and keep our ancestors in chains. But this isn't just a history lesson, it's a reclamation project that proves our African ancestors were leading the church long before a slave ship ever sailed. I love that this book doesn't offer cheap answers but instead gives us the receipts to dismantle the lie that Christianity is just a white man's religion. If you're ready to stop surviving in spaces that don't see you and start thriving in a faith that finally feels like home, you need to read this book.

—Kareem Grimes, actor, *All American*

For the first time in American history, the younger generation of Blacks is leaving the church en masse; it's what sociologists refer to as the "Black exodus." Unable to disentangle the faith of "Big Mama" from that of our enslavers, many have thrown the proverbial baby out with the bathwater.

So what are we to do? I'd start by reading my friend Dr. JP Foster's honest, healing, and hope-filled book *The Gospel and My Black Skin*. When you finish, you will be inspired, as the old folks used to sing in the Black church, to "hold to his hand, God's unchanging hand."

—Dr. Bryan Loritts, author, *Grace to Overcome: Thirty-One Devotions on God's Work Through Black History*

Rev. Dr. JP Foster doesn't pull any punches here. This book strikes a devastating blow to the insidious forms of white supremacy that have flourished under the church's protection. His goal is to help Black readers understand the pain and disappointment they have experienced at the hands of believers who have absorbed forms of racism and used the Bible to justify them. Then he demonstrates that Christianity is not a "white man's religion" but grew robustly in Africa before it did so in Europe. After highlighting Black heroes of the faith, Dr. Foster paints a hopeful picture of a collaborative and healthy future where believers of all races can worship and work together.

Dr. Foster's writing style is effortless to read—powerful prose that will challenge readers of any race to rethink their ideas about where Christianity came from and who shaped it to become what it is today. A prophetic word. A healing balm. An urgent message. Take up and read!

—Dr. Carmen Imes, Associate Professor of Old Testament, Biola University; author, *Bearing God's Name, Being God's Image,* and *Becoming God's Family*

One of my biggest areas of grief as a pastor is that the Bible, the book of truth, throughout history has been hijacked by so many lies. Contrary to what so many people believe, white missionaries didn't bring Christianity to Africa, and people of color have never been an afterthought in the heart of God. What we need now more than ever are the corrective lenses to see the Bible for the truth that it really is. *The Gospel and My Black Skin* provides those lenses. This book is so timely and so needed. Read it and be healed.

—Dr. Van Moody, pastor, The Worship Center Christian Church; author, *The People Factor: How Building Great Relationships and Ending Bad Ones Unlocks Your God-Given Purpose*

The Gospel and My Black Skin

Confronting the Past, Reclaiming the Future

DR. JP FOSTER

ZONDERVAN REFLECTIVE

ZONDERVAN REFLECTIVE

The Gospel and My Black Skin

Published by Zondervan, 3950 Sparks Drive SE, Suite 101, Grand Rapids, MI 49546, USA. Zondervan is a registered trademark of The Zondervan Corporation, L.L.C., a wholly owned subsidiary of HarperCollins Christian Publishing, Inc.

Requests for information should be addressed to customercare@harpercollins.com.

Zondervan titles may be purchased in bulk for educational, business, fundraising, or sales promotional use. For information, please email SpecialMarkets@Zondervan.com.

ISBN 978-0-310-18032-6 (audio)

Library of Congress Cataloging-in-Publication Data

Names: Foster, John-Paul C., 1984- author

Title: The gospel and my Black skin : confronting the past, reclaiming the future / Dr. JP Foster.

Description: Grand Rapids, MI, USA : Zondervan Reflective, [2026] | Includes biographical information. | Includes bibliographical references and index.

Identifiers: LCCN 2025047127 (print) | LCCN 2025047128 (ebook) | ISBN 9780310180302 softcover | ISBN 9780310180319 ebook

Subjects: LCSH: Africa—Church history | Church history—Primitive and early church, ca. 30-600 | Slavery and the church—History | Slavery—Religious aspects—Christianity | Slavery—United States—History | African American churches—History | African Americans—Religious life

Classification: LCC BR563.B53 F67 2026 (print) | LCC BR563.B53 (ebook)

LC record available at https://lccn.loc.gov/2025047127

LC ebook record available at https://lccn.loc.gov/2025047128

HarperCollins Publishers, Macken House, 39/40 Mayor Street Upper, Dublin 1, D01 C9W8, Ireland (https://www.harpercollins.com)

Cover design: Darren Welch Design
Cover image: © Ratchapoom Anupongpan / Getty Images
Interior design: Kristy Edwards

Printed in the United States of America

26 27 28 29 30 LBC 5 4 3 2 1

To my brothers:

Terrence Foster (passed away in 2017)
Junior Foster (passed away in 2021)

Your lives, questions, and our rich
discussions continue to shape this work.
You are deeply missed and forever remembered.

Contents

Foreword by Lisa Victoria Fields xiii

INTRODUCTION: WHAT DO WE DO WITH THIS FAITH? 1

The Journey Ahead 5

Meeting You Where You Are 7

Before We Begin: A Brief Word on Listening 9

Let the Work Begin—with Truth 13

PART 1: BEARING THE WOUND

ONE: WHEN FAITH WAS WEAPONIZED 17

When It Came into Focus for Me 20

The Curse of Ham Was Everywhere 22

Theologians Who Made It Gospel 25

A Gospel Distorted Still 27

TWO: STILL THE MOST SEGREGATED HOUR 31

The Pews Were Never Neutral 34

When Scripture Was Twisted to Defend Segregation 37

They Didn't Just Watch, They Preached It 39

When the Civil Rights Movement Came to Church 42

Redlines and the Cost of Silence 46
The Legacy of Redlining 49
The New Jim Crow 53
When Christianity Gets Wrapped in a Flag 59
Reckoning with What's Already Happened 65

THREE: BLACK AMERICANS ARE LEAVING CHURCH 69
Losing Trust, Leaving Church 72
Not Leaving Jesus, Just What's Been Done in His Name 74
When Power Replaces Compassion 78
Not Just Leaving White Churches 84
When Trust Breaks, Everything Shifts 88

PART 2: BREAKING THE CHAINS

FOUR: RECLAIMING CHRISTIANITY'S AFRICAN ROOTS 95
Africa at the Heart of Early Christianity 99
Meet the African Minds Who Shaped the Faith 101

FIVE: FAITH-FUELED RESISTANCE 127
"Let My People Go": The Faith of Nat Turner 129
Harriet Tubman: A Legacy of Resistance and Liberation 131
The Abolitionist Witness 134
The Civil Rights Movement 136

SIX: THE GOD BEHIND THE RESISTANCE **149**
Justice Is Who God Is 151
Justice at the Heart of Jesus' Mission 154
Justice and the Image of God 156

SEVEN: EVERY PERSON IS MADE IN THE IMAGE OF GOD **159**
The *Imago Dei* in Today's English 162
Universal Human Dignity 163
Impact on Racial Justice 166
Bearing God's Image in the World 170

PART 3: BECOMING THE NEW BODY

EIGHT: ONENESS **173**
What Oneness Really Means 175
There Were Walls in the Bible Too 176
Jesus Tears Down Walls 177
Jesus Started a New Thing 179
The Church as a Community of Reconciliation 184
Living This Out, in You and Through You 185

NINE: HOPE FOR THE FUTURE **189**
A Vision of the True Church Is a New Body 191
A Glimpse of Hope 192
A Personal Witness 193
This Faith Has Always Been Yours 195
This Is Not the End 197

Notes 201

Foreword

RECENTLY, THE JUDE 3 PROJECT SURVEYED students across seven historically Black colleges and universities (Morehouse College, Spelman College, Clark Atlanta University, Florida A&M University, Tuskegee University, Alcorn State University, and Morgan State University) and asked them what their greatest obstacle is to fully embracing Christianity. Across all the campuses, we found the two top responses were consistent: "the way Christianity has been used historically to harm people" and "hypocrisy in the church."

The survey results reflect what I see time after time in my engagement with Black students on campuses, in my conversations with Black young adults who have left the church, and on my social media timeline. Many Black people are wondering whether Christianity is actually good news for them, and it is not hard to see why. A counterfeit Christianity is embedded in the history of Europe and the United States, and the misuse of Bible passages has done significant harm to Black people, especially during slavery and colonialism.

However, a counterfeit can exist only if there is an authentic. When the Christian faith is rightly lived out and the Bible is adequately understood and applied, it's liberating and healing not just for Black people but for all people.

That's why I am so thankful that Dr. John-Paul C. Foster took on the task of writing this book to help people who are struggling to sort through Christianity's complex past and present. Through this book, he exposes counterfeit Christianity for the evil it is, while at the same time shedding light on the liberation and transformation that authentic Christianity brings to Black lives. For years Dr. Foster, a pastor and scholar, has been on the front lines of helping men and women find their way as they try to navigate the damage caused by the misuse and abuse of Scripture, which distorts how they see themselves, the Bible, and God. Throughout the pages of this book, he draws on his experience and research with compassion and conviction to help Black people see who we are and whose we are. In a world ravaged by bad news, Dr. Foster reminds us that the message of Jesus remains good news for Black people.

This good news affirms our Black identity, liberates us from sin, and provides hope. It restores our relationships with God, ourselves, and one another. As you read this book, interrogate the lies you have believed about your worth and value. Take note of the ways you have accepted misinterpretations of the Word of God. Evaluate the ways that you have let the misuse of the Bible detour you from the person the whole Bible is about.

Friend, I know you have been wounded and hurt by

those in the church. I know the history of the faith has created an angst in your soul. Dr. Foster and I see you, and we understand. However, the healing you need and desire is found in a suffering savior named Jesus Christ. Only Jesus has the power to free you from the sin of slavery and the slavery of sin. Let Dr. Foster's words minister to your soul. As you read, invite God in through prayer. You may have walked away from a counterfeit version of Jesus, but allow this book to introduce you to the real him.

—*Lisa Victoria Fields*,
CEO AND FOUNDER, JUDE 3 PROJECT

Introduction

What Do We Do with This Faith?

IT WAS 2021 WHEN I WALKED INTO THE Museum of the Bible in Washington, DC, not just as a pastor or a scholar, but as a Black man with a burden. I wasn't there just for the artifacts or the architecture. I had a question pressing on my spirit—one that wouldn't let me go.

We were halfway through the tour, moving past scrolls and ancient manuscripts, when I couldn't wait any longer. I interrupted the guide mid-sentence.

"Is the Slave Bible here?"

The words left my mouth, and suddenly the air changed. The group tensed. Some looked at the floor. Others stared at me as if I'd said something inappropriate.

The guide gave a quiet nod. "Yes."

That wasn't enough.

"Could you take me to it before we finish the tour?"

Another pause. Then again, "Yes."

That was all I needed.

At that moment, I realized I had become *that* guy—the one who disrupts the flow of the tour, drawing attention to something many people probably didn't even know existed. As we moved along, I could hear the whispers of others wondering why on earth such a Bible would exist.

Finally, he led us to the quiet exhibit. There, behind glass, was a heavily edited Bible from 1807—printed for enslaved Africans in the British West Indies. It wasn't exactly what most people expect, because it appears more like a pamphlet than a whole Bible. Ninety percent of the Old Testament had been cut. Entire books—Exodus, Jeremiah, the psalms of lament—gone. Only fragments remained. The message was clear: a Bible without liberation, without justice, without hope. Just enough Scripture to keep people in chains. A distorted gospel. A weaponized faith.

That wasn't the first time I had learned about the Slave Bible. I had studied it, spoken about it, and even used it in teaching. But standing in front of that glass case—seeing it up close, with entire books stripped out—was a heavy experience. It reminded me that the legacy of this kind of manipulation is more than a historical footnote. It's ongoing. The effects of an edited faith, distorted and weaponized against Black people, are still with us. We are still reckoning with a Christianity that, too often, has been used to dominate rather than deliver.

And so I returned to a question that's sat with me for

years, one I've heard echoed in living rooms, classrooms, church pews, and protest lines: What do we do with this faith?

What do we do with a faith that has been used both to liberate and to oppress? A faith that inspired the courage of Harriet Tubman and Nat Turner but also belonged to slaveholders who claimed Christ while branding their slaves—sometimes marking them with initials, sometimes quoting Scripture as they did it?

What do we do with churches that preached salvation through grace while justifying the ownership of human beings?

We ask this because we're living with the fallout. The wounds are not theoretical—they're personal. And, in our time, more and more Black Christians are asking hard questions about whether this faith is still ours.

A 2021 Pew Research Center study revealed that 28 percent of Black adults under thirty now identify as religiously unaffiliated, compared to just 11 percent of Black adults over sixty-five—a generational shift of seismic proportions.[1] What researchers have called "the Black exodus" is well underway. And while many still believe in Jesus, they're walking away from the institutions that claimed his name but failed to live his love.

Some left quietly. Others stormed out. But the pain runs deep either way. One Barna study reported higher levels of spiritual trauma among Black Christians from churches than any other racial group—pointing not just to racism in the culture but to racism in the pews.[2]

Why is this happening?

Is the church listening?

Listening is the first act of love. But let's be honest—too often, the Black church hasn't been listened to. In moments when we've spoken out, American Christianity—especially our white brothers and sisters—traded listening for defensiveness, empathy for fragility, and repentance for denial. Instead of lamenting, they gaslit us. Instead of repairing, they went silent. When we said we were hurting, they accused us of being divisive. When we told our stories, they changed the subject. And when we talked about justice, they told us to stick to preaching the gospel.

But Jesus never separated justice from the gospel.

When Jesus began his public ministry, he stood up in the synagogue and read from Isaiah: "The Spirit of the Lord is on me, because he has anointed me to proclaim good news to the poor . . . freedom for the prisoners . . . to set the oppressed free" (Luke 4:18).

Did you hear his mission statement? Liberation was front and center.

So how can I still follow Jesus when the religion done in his name has been used to harm me and people like me?

That's the question this book will explore—honestly, theologically, and personally. I won't offer easy answers. But I will point to a faith big enough to hold your questions and bold enough to confront the lies that tried to keep you in chains.

I want to show you that the gospel was never the problem. The gospel is what sets us free.

The Journey Ahead

This book unfolds in three parts. Each section tells a different part of the story—bearing the wound, breaking the chains, and becoming the new body.

Bearing the Wound

We begin in part 1 with the hard truth: Christianity was weaponized against Black people. From the transatlantic slave trade to Jim Crow to mass incarceration, faith was twisted into a tool of control. The so-called curse of Ham was preached as divine justification for white supremacy. In 1867, Southern Presbyterian theologian Robert L. Dabney wrote, "The Scriptures teach clearly the perpetuity of the distinction of races, and the subordination of the inferior." That wasn't a fringe view. It was mainstream theology in Southern pulpits for generations.

To bear the wound is not to wallow in pain—it's to name it. To refuse silence. Before we can begin to heal or reclaim anything, we have to tell the truth about what was done to us—and what was done in God's name. This section invites you to sit with that history, not to stay there forever, but to start the journey in a place of honesty.

We'll trace how white Christians didn't just stay silent—they systematized their beliefs into theologies that upheld slavery, segregation, and incarceration. And in far too many churches those systems still cast shadows today.

We'll also wrestle with the exodus—the painful reality that many Black Americans are leaving the church. Not because they've rejected Jesus, but because they can no longer trust what's been done in his name.

Breaking the Chains

In part 2 we reclaim the story they tried to erase.

To break the chains is to reject the lie that our faith was ever theirs to define. It's to rise from the ashes of stolen history and distorted theology with the courage to remember who we are. This part of the journey is not just about recovery—it's about resistance. It's about reclaiming a faith that was always ours, even when others tried to bury it.

Before colonizers ever set foot on African shores, the gospel had already taken root there. We will look at a short list of the African theologians that helped shape the core doctrines of Christianity. As theologian Thomas C. Oden writes, "Africa played a decisive role in the formation of Christian culture. If one were to remove Africa from the Christian story, it would be a very different story."[3]

We'll explore the deep wells of theology, prayer, and resistance that sustained Black faith through slavery and Jim Crow. We'll revisit heroes such as Fannie Lou Hamer, who said, "We want to be free, because we know that if we don't get up and stand up for our rights, the God we serve is going to make us free."[4] Their faith wasn't naive—it was defiant. And it still has power.

Becoming the New Body

Finally, in part 3 we'll answer the question "Where do we go from here?" We'll turn toward hope. Not just healing from the past, but a vision for the church we can become.

To become the body is to live into the oneness that Christ already made possible. It's not about pretending we're the same—it's about being joined together across difference by the Spirit of God. This part of the journey is about imagining a faith that reflects heaven's diversity and heaven's justice. The church was never meant to be segregated or silent. It was meant to be one.

Reconciliation, as Scripture describes it, isn't a one-time event—it's a way of life. The apostle Paul writes in Ephesians 2 that Christ "has destroyed the barrier, the dividing wall of hostility," making "one new humanity out of the two" (vv. 14–15). That's the invitation: to live into a oneness that doesn't erase difference but honors it in love.

In this final section, we'll explore what that kind of unity looks like in practice. We'll reflect on worship, community, and what it means to belong to one another—not in theory, but in real life. Because the end of this story isn't just about what was taken from us. It's about what we can build together.

Meeting You Where You Are

I'm writing this book for you—the young Black men and women in our churches and neighborhoods who are wrestling with one question: "Why should I trust a faith that's been weaponized against me?" Maybe you're holding on by a thread, wondering whether Jesus still speaks into the pain you've felt. Maybe you left the church years ago, but in your quiet moments you hear a whisper: *Could there be something here worth coming back for?* Or perhaps you've checked out entirely—tired of a Christianity that too often ignored our stories and our suffering.

But I'm also writing for those of you who are *still here*—committed, rooted, showing up with faith intact but questions burning. You believe in Jesus. You love his church. And yet you're looking for truth that won't flinch, for theology that reflects your full humanity, for a deeper understanding of how our story has always been part of God's story. This book is for your equipping and empowerment.

I know the weight you carry: the sermons and seminaries that gloss over your history, the textbooks that erase our brothers and sisters, the fear that opening your Bible will only remind you of how you've been sold—and sold out. I'm not asking you to agree with everything I write. All I ask is that you stay with me. Together we'll name the wrongs done in Christ's name, reclaim the hope hidden in our heritage, and discover a gospel that fights for justice as fiercely as it offers grace.

If you've been burned by the church—if you feel spiritually homeless, skeptical of any message that doesn't match its promise—you're not alone, and this book is for you. I'll give you the words to call out the harm, the stories to remind you of the power, and the road map to imagine a faith that unshackles.

While my primary plea is to you, my brothers and sisters, others may find themselves listening in—pastors desiring to shepherd more faithfully, counselors longing to bring deeper wisdom, seekers drawn to a faith that confronts injustice with integrity and hope. Some may read to better understand our story, to educate themselves about a history too long ignored, or to learn what it means to stand in solidarity. I've woven takeaways for each of you, but know this: My first words are for the young Black man and woman still asking, "Is this faith for me?"

This isn't about blame—it's about truth. It's not about shame—it's about healing. And it's not about losing faith—it's about unshackling it.

Before We Begin: A Brief Word on Listening

Let's be real—when it comes to our faith and our pain, the problem hasn't been that Black people aren't listening.

We've listened. For generations, we've sat through sermons that skipped over our suffering. We've heard prayers that asked for unity but never named injustice. We've had to swallow the silences, the sideways glances, the "let's move on" moments. So no, this chapter isn't here to tell you to listen harder.

It's about making sure *you* feel heard.

Because as we walk through the history of how Christianity has been used to harm our people, I don't want you to read this book as though you're sitting in a classroom. You're not a student here—you're a witness. You carry this history in your bones. Some of these chapters may echo your own story. Others may put words to something you've always felt but never said out loud.

So before we move forward, I want to offer you this: a space to listen—to your own soul.

Not because you haven't been paying attention. But because real healing means tuning in to what's been buried or brushed aside. And real freedom means reclaiming your right to feel, to question, to remember, and to hope.

Here's how I've learned to listen to myself in the middle of all the noise:

When a chapter hits a nerve, let it. Don't rush past the sting. Don't tell yourself to "toughen up" or "just focus on the positive." Sit with it. Let the pain speak. That ache might be the beginning of your healing.

You might feel angry. Or numb. Or affirmed. Whatever rises—welcome it. That response is part of your story. And you don't need to justify it to anyone.

You don't have to agree with everything in these pages. But let the stories land before you decide how you feel about them. That's not about politeness—it's about honoring the depth of what we're carrying.

If you've ever felt dismissed in church or overlooked in faith conversations, this book is your chance to talk back—not to pick a fight, but to reclaim your full humanity. Let what you read here stir questions, memories, prayers. Write in the margins. Cry if you need to. Yell if you need to. This space is yours.

Listening Is the First Act of Love

Dietrich Bonhoeffer once wrote, "Just as our love for God begins with listening to God's word, the beginning of love for other Christians is learning to listen to them."

It's a powerful statement, but let's be honest—too many white Christians never listened. Not to the cries of the enslaved. Not to the sorrow songs. Not to the sermons preached through clenched jaws and weary hope. Not to the generations of Black believers who spoke with conviction about the gospel and justice in the same breath.

And when people don't listen—really listen—pain doesn't go away. It piles up. That's why the ache is still here. Why the anger keeps boiling. Why the silence feels like betrayal. Because for centuries white churches sang about grace while ignoring the groans of their Black siblings. They called for unity but refused to hear the truth that would make unity possible. Listening is the first act of love—and love, as the Bible says, does not dishonor others.

But here's the shift I want to make in this book. This isn't about begging to be heard. Not anymore. You and I come from a people who've learned to carry truth in our bodies even when our voices were ignored. You already know how to hold pain, how to trace hope through heartbreak. You've been listening to stories all your life—at family reunions, in barbershops or salons, in pews where the preacher made you feel seen.

Now it's time to tell your own.

You don't have to be the translator for anyone else. You don't have to prove the depth of your experience. But what you can do—what I hope you will do—is reclaim a posture of truth telling. A posture of honesty that refuses to sugarcoat what you've seen and felt. And when the time comes for others to listen—especially our white brothers and sisters—don't settle for polite nods. Call them deeper. Because real love doesn't whisper around hard truths. It tells the truth in love and then watches who's willing to stay in the room.

You already know how to hold stories.

Now it's time to let someone hold yours.

What If You Encounter Defensiveness?

As you share these hard truths, you'll meet white Christians who feel accused or go on the defensive—and that's where empathy comes in. Their reaction isn't about you personally; it often springs from fear of losing something they hold dear: their faith identity, their family heritage, or their place in the church. The idea that their ancestors, their congregations, or their traditions played a part in racial injustice can trigger guilt, shame, or even anger.

Your call isn't to excuse their defensiveness but to recognize its power and complexity. Remember: Empathy doesn't abandon the need for justice—it strengthens it. When you lean in and say, "I see how hard this is to hear," you create room for honest dialogue. You're not watering down the work of accountability; you're offering a path toward understanding.

This doesn't mean you soften your message. It means you hold firm to truth while extending patience and grace. You listen as you ask them to listen. You model the difficult balance of justice and compassion. In doing so, you open the door for transformation—both in their hearts and in our shared journey toward healing.

Let the Work Begin—with Truth

This book will press on some tender places. It will ask you to wrestle—with history, with Scripture, and with the way faith has been used both to heal and to harm. I won't offer easy answers. But I will offer evidence: stories, scriptures, and receipts. I'll bring what I've seen, what I've studied, and what I've lived—and I'll ask you to weigh it with courage.

Because if our faith is going to mean something real for us—for our families, our churches, our future—it has to start with truth. Not sugarcoated. Not skipped over. But spoken, heard, and held.

This isn't about listening to white guilt or white explanations. It's about listening to your own story. Listening to the Spirit. Listening to the parts of our faith that got buried beneath the noise—and pulling them back into the light.

It might stir up grief. It might stir up rage. It might stir up hope. That's not a sign you're off track. That's how transformation starts.

So if you're ready, not just to believe again, but to believe differently, more honestly, more freely, then let's begin.

PART 1

Bearing the Wound

WE'RE NOT STARTING WITH ANSWERS—we're beginning with the scars. Before healing can come, we must first name the harm. And much of that harm came from people who wore the name of Jesus as a shield while wielding Scripture to justify slavery, racism, and silence.

Part 1 is the hard work. It's the section most would rather skip—especially inside the church. But if you and I are serious about reclaiming a faith that is both true and just, we have to start at what's been done in its name.

This isn't an exercise in sensationalizing trauma or drowning in shame. It's an exercise in clarity. The gospel doesn't launch with comfort—it begins with confrontation. It begins with a God who calls out sin before pouring out grace. That's our task here.

We will trace how the Bible was distorted—how verses were cut, chapters rearranged, and promises twisted—to uphold the enslavement of our African ancestors. We'll name the false theologies preached from pulpits and printed in seminary classrooms. Then we'll follow their echoes through segregation, mass incarceration, and the deep distrust too many Black Christians still carry today.

If you feel uneasy, hold that feeling close. Discomfort can be sacred. If grief rises, let it. It means your heart is open to the truth.

This isn't the complete story—but it is where our story must begin.

When Faith Was Weaponized

A text without context is a pretext for a proof text.
—Unknown

I'LL NEVER FORGET THE DAY MY LATE brother Junior sat me down and told me why he couldn't accept Christianity. We were both younger then, still wrestling with our place in the world and what faith meant to us as Black men. But Junior had already drawn a hard line.

"The Bible was used to enslave us," he said. "How can I trust a book that was weaponized to justify our oppression? Christianity is the white man's religion!"

He wasn't angry—he was heartbroken. And his heartbreak led him elsewhere. To the Nation of Islam. To teachings that gave him dignity, pride, and purpose—but also convinced him that Christianity was the white man's religion, designed to keep Black people submissive and weak.

I didn't have an answer for him that day. I just listened. And in the quiet that followed, something shifted in me. I thought Jesus and the Bible were good and acceptable. But I hadn't yet reckoned with how Jesus and the Scriptures had been twisted to uphold slavery, segregation, and silence.

Junior's words haunted me. They made me question—and they ignited a fire in me to dig deeper, to understand the roots of this faith for myself, and to reclaim what had been stolen.

That conversation didn't push me away from Christianity. It pushed me to study religion for myself. It pushed me to unearth the truth beneath the distortion. Because I had to know: Was there a gospel that could still be good news for people like us? After all, eternity was on the line!

You need to know this right away: The Bible you hold in your hand was not simply read by enslaved Africans—it was carved down, trimmed, and twisted to keep them under control. In 1807 the Society for the Conversion of Negro Slaves in the British West Indies published *Select Parts of the Holy Bible for the Use of the Negro Slaves*—now called the Slave Bible. Its purpose was not to set hearts free but to bind them in obedience.

Staring at that same Slave Bible in the museum exhibit, I felt a knot in my chest. More than 90 percent of the Old

Testament and nearly half of the New had been erased. Exodus—the epic story of Moses leading God's people out of bondage—was gone. Revelation's vision of a new heaven, where "God will wipe away every tear," was gone. Prophets like Isaiah, Amos, and Jeremiah who thundered against injustice were gone. What remained was a skeleton of select chapters—232 instead of 1,189—all chosen to preach submission rather than liberation.

The first passages enslaved people encountered often read like a handbook for servitude. Ephesians 6:5 commanded, "Slaves, obey your earthly masters with respect and fear, and with sincerity of heart, just as you would obey Christ."

Galatians 3:28—"There is neither Jew nor Gentile, neither slave nor free . . . for you are all one in Christ Jesus"—was entirely cut away. Imagine the sting of holding a book that promises unity in Christ only to have that promise snatched from your sight.

By controlling which verses reached enslaved ears, British missionaries and slaveholders shaped a Bible of bondage instead of good news. They preached Joseph's story (Genesis 39)—a narrative of faithful servitude rewarded—to model obedient labor, while erasing his eventual rise and reunion with family. They left in Proverbs on humility but cut out justice, mercy, and God's fury against oppressors.

When I first learned this, I was furious—and ashamed that the church I served and seminary I attended never told me this story. But acknowledging this distortion is the first step toward reclaiming the gospel's full power.

This wasn't a one-off atrocity. It was the natural fruit of a white-supremacist theology that saturates our history. Missionaries didn't just snip out verses with scissors—they preached sermons, wrote commentaries, and shaped seminary curricula to uphold slavery. In America, enslavers forbade full Bibles, fearing that any exposure to freedom texts would spark rebellion.

What you discover in these pages is that the gospel is nothing like the Slave Bible's message. Real good news is that God liberates the oppressed, tears down every wall of division, and calls us into radical equality and justice.

Hold that tension: grief over what was lost and hope for what can be restored. Let the knowledge of the Slave Bible's cruelty fuel your hunger for the uncut, unshackled Word. As we move deeper into part 1, we'll trace how these edited truths echoed through segregation, Jim Crow, and mass incarceration—and how, even today, the legacy of a manipulated gospel still affects us.

Remember: Confronting this wound is not sensationalism—it's clarity. Our faith begins with naming sin before we taste grace. And it begins here.

When It Came into Focus for Me

I wasn't looking for a fight that day—I just wanted lunch.

I had ducked into the campus diner between classes, books still under my arm, when I ran into a faculty member. We got to talking, and I mentioned—almost in passing—that

I had started doing some personal research into how Christianity had been used to justify slavery. I expected maybe a nod or a general affirmation. But instead he paused, looked me straight in the eye, and said, "Have you read about the curse of Ham?"

I hadn't. Not in depth. I'd heard whispers of it, vague references to some passage in Genesis, but I didn't know the full weight of it. So he gave me some resources—book recommendations and key scholars and theologians—and said, "Start there."

What I found wrecked me.

I read how theologians and preachers for centuries took a passage about when Noah's son Ham saw his father naked and twisted it into a justification for Black inferiority. I saw how they claimed God had cursed an entire people, how they tied Blackness itself to divine punishment, how they used Scripture not just to defend slavery but to normalize it.

And I realized something I hadn't fully faced before: This wasn't just a bad interpretation. It was deliberate. Calculated. A theological system built to support a racial caste.

It made me sick.

That day in the diner was the start of a deeper journey for me—not just into historical theology but into reckoning. I had always believed the Bible was true. But now I had to ask—whose truth had been taught? Whose truth had been erased?

Because this wasn't just an intellectual discovery. It was a spiritual betrayal. And I needed to know whether the gospel I had given my life to could still be trusted.

The Curse of Ham Was Everywhere

At the heart of the theological distortion that fueled racial slavery was the so-called curse of Ham—a misreading of Genesis 9:20–27 that evolved into one of the most enduring religious justifications for Black enslavement.

In the biblical account, Noah cursed Canaan, the son of Ham, declaring: "Cursed be Canaan! The lowest of slaves will he be to his brothers" (Gen. 9:25). Note that Ham himself was not cursed. The text never mentions race, never references Africa, and never describes skin color. Yet over the centuries this passage was twisted into a doctrine of divine racial hierarchy. Preachers, theologians, and politicians reimagined the curse as falling on all of Ham's descendants—who were assumed to have populated Africa—and claimed it as God's eternal judgment on Black people.

By the seventeenth century, the curse of Ham theology had gained legal traction. In 1667 the Virginia General Assembly passed a law declaring that baptism would not free enslaved Africans—firmly linking race, slavery, and Christian theology in colonial policy.

And it wasn't just in the colonies. Across the Atlantic, a myth was solidifying. David M. Whitford writes that the curse of Ham "was a Christian invention . . . the invention of a theological rationale for the Atlantic slave trade."[1] According to Whitford, it did not emerge directly out of the need for slaves, but rather it became useful as defenders of slavery sought to legitimize it in the face of growing critique. To have utility, it had to carry cultural currency—and that currency was forged through pulpits, pamphlets, popular commentary, and raw political power.

This myth endured into the twentieth century. On June 10, 1964, as the US Senate debated the Civil Rights Act, Senator Robert C. Byrd—a former Klan member—stood for more than fourteen hours in the longest filibuster in Senate history (a record later surpassed in 2025 by Senator Cory Booker during a protest of voting rights legislation). In his closing remarks, Byrd turned to Genesis 9. He had searched the Bible, he claimed, and found "no scriptural basis" for civil rights legislation. Instead, he read Genesis 9:18–27 into the *Congressional Record* as divine sanction for racial separation.[2]

Such readings were not fringe. They were deeply rooted into the culture of the United States and clearly articulated by pastors in the South. Robert L. Dabney wrote after the Civil War, "The Scriptures teach clearly the perpetuity of the distinction of races, and the subordination of the inferior."[3]

He was not dismissed as a radical. Dabney was a seminary professor, a former Confederate chaplain, and a key figure in the shaping of Southern Presbyterian doctrine. His views were embedded in seminary curricula and Sunday sermons alike.

In 1851, the *Biblical Repertory and Princeton Review* published Charles Hodge's defense of slavery as a "divinely appointed relationship," claiming it was neither unjust nor un-Christian.[4] Hodge wasn't a Southern firebrand—he was a respected Northern theologian, teaching at Princeton Theological Seminary.

Scottish preacher John Brown's *Self-Interpreting Bible*—a popular layperson's commentary published in 1778—stated that for "four thousand years . . . the bulk of Africans have been abandoned of Heaven to the most gross ignorance, rigid slavery, stupid idolatry, and savage barbarity."[5] In his commentary on Genesis 9:25, Brown confidently affirmed the servitude of Black people as a biblical truth.

And in 1851, the Reverend Josiah Priest declared in *Bible Defence of Slavery*, "One of the great facts of God's jurisprudence among men appears to be the judicial appointment of the black race to slavery." He rooted this argument in the belief that Noah's curse on Ham was not merely prophecy but God's binding judicial decree, entailing perpetual servitude on people of African descent. The curse upon the descendants of Ham was a curse of servitude . . . a dark race were designed to serve."[6]

David M. Whitford, historian and author, traces the roots of this theology to both ancient and fabricated sources. He points to forged "histories," such as those by Annius of Viterbo, which blended Greco-Roman mythology, medieval superstition, and political ambition. In the 1750s, Church of England bishop Thomas Newton offered a notorious defense of the curse of Ham by selectively and knowingly distorting biblical sources—ignoring more than two centuries of critical examination to uphold racial hierarchy.[7]

Over time, Ham became mythologized as the root of all behavior opposed to God, order, and civilization. As Whitford explains, "Ham became the primary mover behind all things opposed to God, the church, or proper behavior."[8]

Darkness of skin was equated with darkness of spirit. People of African descent were cast as natural rebels against God's design, a lie that laid spiritual justification for centuries of dehumanization.

But this wasn't simply poor interpretation. It was theological malpractice—what Whitford calls a "Frankenstein creation" of fragments stitched together from "medieval exegetes, classical authors, propaganda, necessity, and greed."[9]

In the words of theologian Stephen Haynes, "this myth played a central role in antebellum justifications for American slavery."[10] It became more than a textual misreading—it became the theological architecture that made racism sacred.

The residue of this distortion remains with us today. Churches may no longer preach about Ham from the pulpit, but the effects linger in systems that remain blind to racial injustice, in institutions that treat African Christianity as marginal, and in discipleship that forms piety without equity.

This was not the gospel of Jesus Christ. It was a manipulated gospel that served power instead of truth. A gospel of chains, not liberation.

Theologians Who Made It Gospel

What began as a myth and progressed into a deliberate misinterpretation of Genesis 9 eventually became doctrinal scaffolding for white Christian supremacy. The curse of Ham wasn't just whispered in private—it was preached from pulpits, taught at seminaries, printed in catechisms, and embedded into the founding charters of denominations.

In 1845, the Southern Baptist Convention was born out of the conviction that slaveholding was not only permissible for missionaries—it was biblically defensible. Their separation from Northern Baptists was political and theological. Slavery, they argued, was sanctioned by Scripture and essential to gospel work among the "uncivilized."[11]

Across the South, this racialized theology was echoed by other denominations. Episcopal bishop Stephen Elliott of Georgia, speaking at the height of the Civil War, declared, "Slavery was established by decree of Almighty God. . . . It is sanctioned in the Bible, in both Testaments, from Genesis to Revelation."[12]

In Presbyterian circles, pro-slavery arguments weren't confined to fiery preachers—they were institutionalized in respected publications. The *Southern Presbyterian Review* regularly published essays defending the enslavement of Africans as a "natural" and "providential" ordering of society, ordained by God's sovereignty.[13]

These were not rogue opinions. They were systemic assertions—found in doctrinal statements, seminary lectures, and church-sponsored pamphlets—designed to reassure slaveholding Christians that their faith and their economy were aligned.

British missionary efforts, too, were shaped by this theology. Many missionaries in the Caribbean taught enslaved Africans only selected Bible passages—those reinforcing obedience and submission—while deliberately avoiding the liberating themes of exodus or the prophetic calls for justice. In doing so, they mirrored the theological strategy of the Slave Bible: curate the gospel to control the people.[14] This gospel distortion wielded Scripture not for transformation but for domination.

These theological systems didn't simply accommodate racism. They sanctified it. They baptized social hierarchy, wrapped inequality in religious language, and turned prejudice into piety. And while the faces of these theologians may be unfamiliar to most today, their legacy lingers in the liturgies, curricula, and inherited assumptions of Western Christianity.

But theological distortion doesn't stay confined to history books or archived sermons. The systems built by these theologians left more than stained pages—they left spiritual residue. Even when the names are forgotten and the arguments abandoned, the frameworks they built echo in today's churches. Which brings us to the present moment.

A Gospel Distorted Still

I'd like to say that all of this is behind us. That the distortions used to justify slavery were buried with the Confederacy. That the curse of Ham, the edited Bibles, the sermons defending bondage were relics of a darker age. But you know as well as I do that the residue remains.

Black Christians still hear echoes in sermons that reduce racial inequality to "individual responsibility," ignoring centuries of policy, violence, and exclusion. We can still hear the faint voice of the Slave Bible in churches that preach submission but stay silent on injustice. And we still feel the legacy of theological segregation in seminary syllabi that extol the church fathers while erasing their African identity—or, if we are lucky, they treat African Christianity as a footnote, not a foundation.

It lingers in discipleship models that prize piety over equity, in mission strategies that export Western norms as if they were the gospel itself, and in the instinct to label justice as "political" while treating privilege as neutral.

And, perhaps most painfully, it shows up in churches that claim to be "colorblind." Churches that speak of unity but resist confession. That welcome diversity in the pews but not in leadership. That teach reconciliation without repair.

This is what happens when theology is shaped to serve the status quo. When the gospel is domesticated to protect power, not confront it.

And the watching world can tell.

This isn't just about historical wrongs—it's about present-day formation. It's about what happens when the people who claim to represent Christ reflect everything he stood against. When the cross is stripped of its call to justice and reduced to a symbol of private comfort.

Which is why the work ahead isn't just sociological. It's theological.

We'll explore that further in the next chapter, as we examine how white Christian leaders didn't just remain silent during segregation and mass incarceration—they built theological systems to defend it. From the pulpit to the policy table, we'll trace how the distortion of the gospel didn't disappear after slavery—it evolved.

But for now it's enough to say this: When the gospel is distorted, people don't just get confused. They get hurt.

And when they walk away, it's not because they've rejected Christ—it's because they can no longer recognize him in the communities that claim his name.

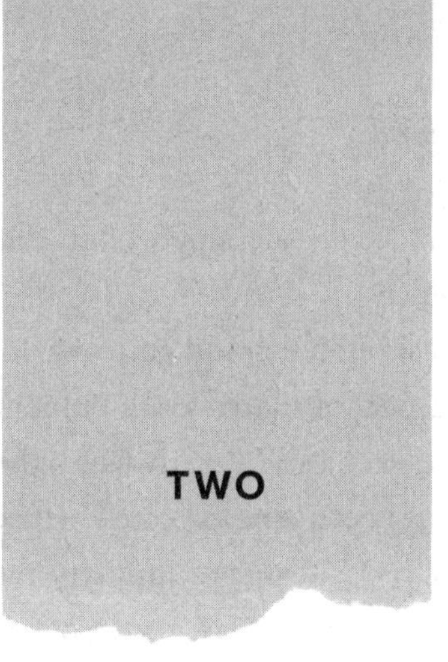

TWO

Still the Most Segregated Hour

I REMEMBER THE MOMENT I SAW IT break his heart.

Bishop Kenneth Ulmer, my spiritual father and one of the most faithful leaders I've ever known, had spent decades building bridges across racial lines. He ministered alongside white pastors, shared conference stages, and collaborated on community projects that affected thousands. He didn't just preach unity—he lived it.

But after George Floyd was murdered, something changed. Or, rather, something was revealed.

Days passed. Then weeks. And from the very people he'd walked so closely with—nothing. No phone call. No text. No public statement. No private support. Just silence. Deafening, devastating silence.

He wasn't asking for grand gestures. Just acknowledgment. Just a moment of shared grief. But it never came.

And I could see it all over his face—the weight of that betrayal. Not just because he expected better, but because he had hoped that years of shared ministry meant something deeper. But when the world was crying out, his friends acted as if nothing had happened. As if George Floyd's death was just another news story. As if our pain wasn't real.

Watching him sit with that silence marked me. It reminded me that no matter how much we serve, how faithfully we lead, or how deeply we invest in reconciliation, there are moments when being Black in white Christian spaces feels like shouting into the wind. You can be respected, even admired. But when the cries of your community go unheard, you start to wonder, *Do they see me, or just what I do for them?*

As respected and prolific as my "Pops" is, I knew he wouldn't stay silent. And, sure enough, on Sunday morning Bishop Ulmer preached one of the most powerful sermons I've ever witnessed—a message that echoed across the nation. Holding a massive black Bible in his hand, he looked straight into the camera and said to his white friends and colleagues, "You don't look like your picture." Then he pointed to the Bible and repeated it, slower this time: "You. Don't. Look. Like. Your. Picture."

It was a son's proudest moment—watching his father stand up for truth, knowing full well it would cost him.

And then came the line that took me out completely. Bishop Ulmer said, "Don't worry about uninviting me or taking me off your engagement list—because I ain't going!"

That moment did something in me. It named a frustration I had carried silently for too long—a gap between the Christianity I read in Scripture and the Christianity I saw defended in public. And it stirred something else too: a fresh resolve. Because I knew I couldn't just admire that kind of courage—I had to live it.

Weekly I stand at the pulpit of my predominantly Black church looking out at faces I've known for years—mothers who raised their children in the pews, elders whose prayers helped shape my own faith, young people still deciding what they believe. The choir's singing concludes, the Spirit is moving. And I'm reminded of a complicated truth.

It's Sunday morning.

And yet, decades after the Civil Rights Movement, most churches in America remain segregated by race.

In a *Meet the Press* interview on April 17, 1960, Dr. King remarked, "Eleven o'clock on Sunday morning is one of the most segregated hours, if not the most segregated hour, in Christian America."[1] More than sixty years later, the observation still holds. In a 2022 study, Lifeway Research found that 76 percent of Protestant pastors say their churches are predominantly one racial or ethnic group, a sobering confirmation that the "most segregated hour in Christian America" has changed far less than many would like to believe.[2]

This isn't just about worship style or cultural preference. Something deeper is at work.

As a pastor, I've wrestled with the history of the American church—especially its role in racial injustice. And if I'm being honest, what I've found is painful. Many white churches didn't just stay silent during moments of racial crisis—they were active participants in the systems of oppression. They defended slavery from the pulpit. They baptized segregation in theological language. They built a Christianity that could exclude the very people it claimed to love.

It's not easy to say that out loud. But it's the truth. And if we're ever going to move forward, we have to be willing to tell the truth about where the church has been and why it hasn't changed enough.

The Pews Were Never Neutral

During the Jim Crow era—roughly from the 1870s to the 1960s—Black Americans lived under a brutal system of racial apartheid. These laws segregated schools, buses, neighborhoods, lunch counters, and even water fountains. But this wasn't just about public policy. It was a theological crisis too. Because much of this system was upheld—or, at the very least, tolerated—by the white church.

Sermons preached in the South cited Acts 17:26—"From one man he made all the nations . . . and he marked out their appointed times in history and the boundaries of their lands"—as biblical support for segregation, arguing that God intended racial groups to remain separate.[3] Segregation, in this distorted theology, wasn't a betrayal of the gospel. It was presented as its fulfillment.

In his 1960 pamphlet *Is Segregation Scriptural?* Bob Jones Sr., the founder of Bob Jones University, declared, "If you are against segregation and against racial separation, then you are against God Almighty."[4] He was not an outlier. His words echoed the broader posture of white evangelicals in that era. Public opinion surveys confirm how deeply rooted this resistance was. In 1963, a Gallup poll found that 60 percent of Americans believed civil rights demonstrations were harming the cause of racial equality, while only 27 percent thought they were helping.[5] Historians underscore that white evangelicals in the South were no exception; indeed, they were among the most resistant to civil rights and integrated worship.[6]

Let me be clear: This does not mean that every white Christian or every white church chose silence. There were courageous allies—white clergy and laypeople who stood alongside Black leaders, marched across the Edmund Pettus Bridge, registered voters in the Mississippi Delta, and suffered real consequences for their convictions. Their faith led them to the front lines. And they should be honored.

But we must also tell the fuller story: Those voices were too often the exception, not the rule.

Most white churches either remained neutral or outright opposed the Civil Rights Movement. Dr. King himself lamented this in his 1963 "Letter from Birmingham Jail," in which he expressed deep disappointment in "the white moderate" who "prefers a negative peace which is the absence of tension to a positive peace which is the presence of justice."

King wasn't just criticizing politicians. He was talking to the white pastors who urged him to "wait," who condemned his tactics while ignoring his message, who preached peace but refused to risk comfort for justice.[7]

The tragedy is that many churches taught their people how to be "respectable" but not how to be righteous.

It wasn't until the moral force of the Civil Rights Movement—rooted largely in the Black church—shook the conscience of the nation that a real reckoning began. Leaders such as Dr. King, Fannie Lou Hamer, and John Lewis, along with countless others whose names we'll never know, called America to repent. They sang spirituals in jail cells and quoted Scripture on the steps of the Lincoln Memorial. They led a theological revival in the streets—insisting that justice is not optional for followers of Jesus.

And yet here we are, decades later, with many churches still hesitant to speak about race.

Some have taken meaningful steps. But too many have settled for a cosmetic diversity or remained silent altogether. And silence is never neutral. We may have ended legal segregation, but people are still being shut out in practice—it's just harder to see now.

If I'm honest, I still hear echoes of those old justifications today. Not in burning crosses or shouted slurs, but in subtle deflections:

- "Let's not get political."
- "Preach the gospel, not social issues."
- "Talking about race just divides the church."

The truth I've had to wrestle with as a pastor is that the pews were never neutral. They were shaped by the theology preached from the pulpit. And when that theology baptized the status quo, it didn't just fail to challenge injustice—it helped sustain it.

When Scripture Was Twisted to Defend Segregation

Throughout American history, white churches and theologians misused Scripture to justify racial segregation and uphold white supremacy. Some of the most egregious distortions came from well-respected religious leaders and institutions.

Acts 17:26 was commonly cited to support segregation. Paul declares, "From one man he made all the nations, that they should inhabit the whole earth; and he marked out their appointed times in history and the boundaries of their lands." This verse affirms the shared origin and dignity of all humanity. But segregationist theologians weaponized it. They zeroed in on the phrase about "boundaries," arguing that God intended racial groups to remain separate—socially, politically, and ecclesiastically. Integration, according to segregationists, was socially disruptive and spiritually rebellious.[8]

The story of the Tower of Babel in Genesis 11 was similarly twisted. Instead of interpreting the narrative as a warning against human arrogance and the pursuit of self-glorification, segregationist preachers argued that God's scattering of the people was divine proof that mixing races was sinful. In their telling, Babel was not a judgment against pride—it was a blueprint for permanent racial separation.[9]

These distortions were reinforced in sermons, seminary lectures, denominational statements, and Christian school curricula throughout the South. In other words, they were mainstream. Following the *Brown v. Board* decision in 1954, Mississippi's White Citizens' Council published and distributed G. T. Gillespie's *A Christian View of Segregation*, which argued that "the Confusion of Tongues, which took place at Babel, with the consequent scattering of the peoples, was an act of special Divine Providence to frustrate the mistaken efforts of godless men to assure the permanent integration of the peoples of the earth."[10] The Citizens' Council distributed such literature widely across the South, with their newspaper alone reaching a print run of 125,000 copies by the mid-1950s.[11]

The theological scaffolding of white supremacy was built with selective proof texts and sanctified by repetition. The so-called curse of Ham, which we explored in the previous chapter, had laid a foundation. But these additional distortions turned the edifice into a fortress—one that many white Christians felt justified in defending as holy ground.

And the effects were not abstract. These interpretations shaped generations of white Christians to see segregation as divinely ordained and racial inequality as part of God's providential order. As theologian James Cone once wrote, "White theologians made God in their image and expected Black people to accept a gospel that dehumanized them."[12]

When Scripture is twisted to approve and justify injustice, the result isn't just bad theology—it's generational harm masquerading as God's divine will.

They Didn't Just Watch, They Preached It

White churches were not passive bystanders in the story of American segregation—they were often architects of it. From the earliest days of American Christianity, Black believers were pushed to the margins of church life. In many white congregations, they were expected to worship in segregated galleries, denied leadership roles, and routinely humiliated—even during sacred moments. One of the most painful expressions of this exclusion came at the Communion table: Black members were often forced to wait until white congregants had received the Lord's Supper—if they were permitted to receive it at all.

A particularly egregious moment occurred in 1816 at Saint George's Methodist Episcopal Church in Philadelphia. Richard Allen, a formerly enslaved preacher and gifted evangelist, had been leading early morning prayer meetings for Black congregants. One Sunday, as Black members knelt to pray, white trustees interrupted the service to forcibly remove them from the sanctuary. Allen later recalled being told mid-prayer to "get up and move." When they refused to be dishonored any further, Allen and others walked out. "We all went out of the church in a body," he wrote, "and they were no more plagued with us in the church."[13]

That act of collective resistance gave birth to the African Methodist Episcopal (AME) Church—the first independent Black denomination in the United States. In 1816, Allen and other Black leaders formally organized the church, elected Allen as its first bishop, and established a space where Black Christians could worship, lead, and minister without white oversight or oppression. The AME Church wasn't just an institution. It was a declaration—a theological and social statement that affirmed the full dignity of Black believers. It became both a sanctuary for faith and a blueprint for what would later be known as the Black church: a prophetic voice that stood firm in the face of racial injustice.

But the white church's theological exclusion didn't end in the nineteenth century—it evolved.

During the Jim Crow era, white churches were not neutral. Many were active participants in preserving the racial order. While some Christians did resist, far more chose to defend the status quo—shaping both public theology and private practice to keep segregation in place. Across the South, churches not only resisted integration but punished those who challenged it. On Easter Sunday 1964 in Jackson, Mississippi, three Black men—including a minister—were barred from entering white churches. When they persisted, ushers blocked the doors and police arrested them.[14] White church members who supported civil rights fared no better. In Mississippi, the 1963 Born of Conviction statement—signed by twenty-eight young white Methodist pastors—publicly opposed segregation. The backlash was swift: Within months, eighteen of the pastors had been forced to leave the state under pressure from segregationists in their congregations and communities.[15] Following the 1954 Supreme Court decision *Brown v. Board of Education*, which declared segregated public schools unconstitutional, many white Christians did not respond with repentance—they responded with resistance. Rather than integrate, they built a network of private schools, often called "segregation academies," which they defended as expressions of "religious freedom" or "parental choice." By the late 1960s, more than two hundred thousand white students in the South were enrolled in these institutions, many openly affiliated with churches.[16]

Pastors preached sermons condemning integration as unbiblical and unnatural. They invoked verses such as 2 Corinthians 6:14—"Do not be unequally yoked" (ESV)—to oppose interracial marriage, and misused Old Testament purity laws to argue against racial mixing. These weren't fringe interpretations. They were proclaimed from pulpits, printed in bulletins, and defended at denominational gatherings.

In many communities, the White Citizens' Councils—a network of white supremacist organizations formed in 1954—drew their leadership from local church deacons and elders. Unlike the Ku Klux Klan, the Councils didn't hide in the shadows. They positioned themselves as respectable defenders of Christian civilization, publishing newsletters, hosting lectures, and circulating theological defenses of segregation. Their meetings were often held in church fellowship halls.[17]

But the problem wasn't just with sermons. It was with systems. White churches built entire ecosystems around exclusion. They designed sanctuaries without any intention of integrating worship. They developed discipleship programs that ignored racial justice. They hired pastors who would protect the culture of the congregation, not challenge it.

Even denominations that prided themselves on being "Bible believing" failed to confront this hypocrisy. They upheld the authority of Scripture while ignoring its demands for justice, reconciliation, and the full dignity of every person made in God's image. In too many places, what counted as "faithfulness to the Bible" was really faithfulness to cultural comfort.

As theologian and historian Jemar Tisby puts it, "The Christian identity of many Americans was inextricably bound to the maintenance of white supremacy. The Bible was interpreted through the lens of racial caste, and Jesus was conscripted into the service of segregation."[18]

This was not a season of unfortunate silence. It was a period of active theological distortion—where exclusion wasn't just tolerated, it was preached. It was taught. It was treated as righteousness.

When the Civil Rights Movement Came to Church

The Civil Rights Movement didn't just confront the laws of the land—it confronted the soul of the church. Dr. King and other faith-rooted leaders weren't simply demanding new legislation. They were calling Christians to live what they preached—to let the gospel speak with power about justice, reconciliation, and the sacred worth of every human being.

For many white churches, that call was too costly. In his now famous "Letter from Birmingham Jail," King offered a devastating critique, not of white supremacists, but of white moderates. He wrote, "I must confess that over the past few years I have been gravely disappointed with the white moderate . . . who is more devoted to 'order' than to justice; who prefers a negative peace which is the absence of tension to a positive peace which is the presence of justice."[19]

He spoke directly to white clergymen who had told him to slow down, to wait, to pursue justice in ways that wouldn't disrupt the status quo. These pastors—many of them devout in their theology—believed that unity meant avoiding hard truths, and that faithfulness meant staying silent in the face of injustice.

Some white Christians did show up. Episcopal seminarian Jonathan Daniels was martyred in Alabama for his work in the movement. White Catholic priests, Protestant pastors, and Jewish rabbis marched in Selma and joined voter-registration drives in Mississippi. These believers risked their reputations—and, in some cases, their lives—to stand in solidarity with Black sisters and brothers. Their courage should be remembered and honored.[20]

But these allies were the exception. The overwhelming pattern was resistance or withdrawal.

Major white denominations struggled—or outright refused—to confront the moral urgency of the movement.

The Southern Baptist Convention, then the largest Protestant denomination in the United States, issued no official support for civil rights during the 1960s. In fact, it wouldn't formally apologize for its historical defense of slavery and racism until 1995—more than thirty years after the passage of the Civil Rights Act.[21]

Other denominations attempted to issue statements of support but faced such internal backlash that they watered them down or shelved them entirely. Many white pastors dismissed the movement as "too political" or "divisive," encouraging their congregations to pray for peace but not to march for justice. Some framed the call for civil rights as a distraction from the church's "spiritual mission," warning that activism threatened the purity of the gospel.

And, all the while, Black Christians were told to wait. To be patient. To trust that change would come in God's time.

Pastors preached sermons about heaven but ignored the hell of discrimination and segregation. They taught about forgiveness but never repented for their silence. And when Black members challenged the status quo, they were often met with discipline—or dismissal.

Entire churches split or closed their doors rather than accept integrated worship. In Mississippi, the white members of the First Baptist Church of Jackson voted in 1964 to rescind the pastor's invitation to a group of Black students who had been quietly attending services. Their presence, they argued, was "divisive."[22]

These choices—the silence, the sermons, the expulsions—were not neutral. They made white churches complicit in sustaining injustice. While Black churches were nurturing the spiritual backbone of the movement—holding strategy meetings, organizing transportation, singing freedom songs—many white churches were actively undermining the call for justice from within.

And as Black churches stepped into that prophetic role, they bore the weight not only of leadership but of retaliation. The Black church has never just been a place of worship—it has been a center of resistance, education, and community organizing. And because of that it has also been a target. During the civil rights era, Black churches across the United States became frequent sites of white violence aimed at silencing protest and instilling fear.

In the early hours of August 15, 1966, just five weeks after it opened its doors in an all-white neighborhood of Providence, Rhode Island, Holy Cross Church of God in Christ was firebombed. Three incendiary devices were thrown through the windows, igniting pews in a Sunday school classroom and shattering the church's newly installed glass. Outside, vandals spray-painted a racial slur on one of the church's pillars.[23]

This act of violence didn't happen in isolation. It occurred amid widespread resistance to racial integration in Providence—at the time one of the most segregated cities in the nation. Nearly 80 percent of Black residents were concentrated in South Providence, and a 1965 study by the University of Rhode Island found the city's segregation levels comparable to those in the Deep South.[24]

Holy Cross wasn't alone. Between 1954 and 1968, nearly

one hundred Black churches across the South were struck by arson or bombing, many of them serving as central meeting places for civil rights organizing.[25] The most infamous of these attacks occurred on September 15, 1963, when members of the Ku Klux Klan planted dynamite under the steps of Birmingham's Sixteenth Street Baptist Church, killing four young Black girls—Addie Mae Collins, Denise McNair, Carole Robertson, and Cynthia Wesley.[26]

Northern cities such as Philadelphia, Seattle, and Providence also saw coordinated acts of terror against Black congregations. A 1996 congressional report noted that these attacks often intensified when Black churches challenged racial segregation in housing, education, or employment.[27]

These assaults were not random—they were strategic. Black churches weren't simply spiritual sanctuaries. They were movement headquarters, safe havens, voter-registration hubs, and rallying points for civil rights leaders. That made them dangerous in the eyes of those who wanted to maintain white supremacy and racial hierarchy.

Redlines and the Cost of Silence

Although many churches eventually acknowledged the sin of segregation in public accommodations, far fewer were willing to examine how racial injustice had shaped the neighborhoods they lived in, the schools they sent their children to, and the wealth they inherited. The fight for justice didn't end when the marches stopped—it moved into the structures that remained untouched. And housing was one of the most powerful of them all.

Economic injustice didn't happen by accident—and the church wasn't just a bystander. It often stood by in silence. Sometimes it even lent its moral weight to the harm. My first lesson about redlining didn't come from textbooks—I learned about it from my father.

I was an adult when I first learned what my father had to do just to buy the house I grew up in.

It didn't come up in a lecture or a history book. It came up one night over dinner, when we were talking about how hard it had been to find good housing back in the day. My dad leaned back in his chair, looked me square in the eye, and said, "They were fine with everything—until they realized I was a Black man."

He had the income. The credit. The down payment. But once the sellers figured out he wasn't white, the deal almost fell apart. They stalled. Made excuses. Tried to back out. It took a fight—not just persistence, but strategy and pressure—for my father to secure that home. The one we laughed in. The one where we held birthdays and holiday celebrations. The one that gave me stability growing up.

I never looked at that house the same after that conversation. It wasn't just a blessing—it was a battle won.

And what broke me most was this: He wasn't bitter. He wasn't angry. He was matter-of-fact. As if that kind of injustice was just a part of the air they breathed. But I felt the anger he didn't name. The quiet weight of knowing my parents had to fight to live in peace—and that the church, by and large, had nothing to say about it.

I started to look around differently. I began to understand why certain neighborhoods looked the way they did, why certain families had to start over again and again, why so many of our elders carried exhaustion in their bodies. This wasn't just economics. It was exclusion. And the people who preached "blessings" on Sundays often stayed silent about the systems that kept those blessings out of reach for us.

What my father experienced had a name: redlining.

It wasn't just one seller's prejudice—it was a widespread, government-sanctioned policy that carved up American cities, deciding which neighborhoods deserved investment and which ones didn't. The dividing line, more often than not, was race. A 1930s map from the Home Owners' Loan Corporation labeled Black neighborhoods "hazardous," drawing literal red lines around them. Banks used those maps to deny home loans. Insurance companies used them to hike premiums. Real estate agents steered Black families away from "good" neighborhoods—and into ones already starved of resources.

One of those communities was Altadena, California, just north of Pasadena. Though recently devastated by the Eden wildfires in 2025, Altadena also bears the legacy of racial exclusion and resistance. Like many other Black enclaves in Los Angeles County, Altadena became a safe haven during the Great Migration—when more than six million African Americans fled the South between 1915 and 1970 to escape violence and oppression. As Isabel Wilkerson writes in

The Warmth of Other Suns, "The Great Migration was an unrecognized immigration within the country, a seeking of political asylum from the repression of Jim Crow."[28] Seeking opportunity, dignity, and freedom, they brought with them deep faith, strong family bonds, and the determination to build something new.

Yet even in cities like Los Angeles, Black migrants faced systemic housing discrimination. Redlining, restrictive covenants, and discriminatory lending practices kept them out of wealthier, white neighborhoods. As a result, Altadena emerged as one of the few places where Black families could own property and build community. It was not a handout—it was carved out through perseverance and resistance.

For many Black families, owning a home in Altadena was about more than shelter—it was about legacy. It represented a foothold in an economy designed to shut them out. And for the Black church, these neighborhoods became more than places of worship. They were places of organizing, resilience, and vision—proof that Black life could thrive even in the shadow of injustice.

The Legacy of Redlining

In the 1930s, amid the Great Depression, the federal government created the Home Owners' Loan Corporation (HOLC) to stabilize the housing market. HOLC produced color-coded maps of American cities, grading neighborhoods by perceived investment risk. Predominantly Black neighborhoods were consistently marked in red—labeled "hazardous"—and made ineligible for federally backed loans. This practice, now known as redlining, systematically excluded Black families from homeownership and generational wealth.[29]

The Federal Housing Administration reinforced this segregation by refusing to insure mortgages in and near Black neighborhoods, while incentivizing white families to purchase homes in newly constructed suburbs. These developments often included racially restrictive covenants, barring Black residents and other people of color from buying homes even if they could afford them.[30]

This was more than a financial decision—it was social engineering backed by federal policy. The consequences rippled outward: White families were able to build equity, pass down assets, and accumulate economic security. Black families were locked out.

White churches didn't create redlining, but many benefited from it. As white congregants moved to the suburbs, churches followed. Those that remained behind in the "redlined" neighborhoods were often under-resourced and overlooked. And too many of the churches that moved said little about the injustice. Some even gave it moral cover, using language like "preserving community values" or "maintaining neighborhood character," as if Christian witness stopped at the church parking lot.

Meanwhile, Black churches remained anchors of faith and resistance in communities burdened by disinvestment. They preached hope in neighborhoods that banks had abandoned and policymakers had forgotten.

The impact of redlining is not just history—it's legacy. A 2017 study by the Federal Reserve found that the average white family in the United States holds nearly eight times the wealth of the average Black family.[31] This gap isn't simply about income—it's about accumulated advantage. Who got a mortgage in 1955? Who built equity? Who could borrow against that equity to send a child to college, start a business, or survive a crisis?

These aren't abstract questions. The effects are still being felt today.

In 2021, Carlette Duffy, a Black woman in Indianapolis, sought to refinance her home in a historic Black neighborhood. After extensive renovations, she expected a significant increase in value. But the first appraisal came back at just $125,000. The second one was even lower. Suspicious, she removed all signs of her identity and asked a friend's white husband to pose as the homeowner for a third appraisal. The result? A valuation of $259,000—more than double the original estimate. "It sinks in," she said, "that what was devaluing my home was me."[32]

That same year, a similar story made headlines on the West Coast. Paul Austin and Tenisha Tate-Austin, a Black couple in Marin City, California, had their newly renovated home appraised at $995,000—nearly $500,000 less than a previous valuation just months earlier. Believing race played a role, they "whitewashed" their home and had a white friend stand in for the next appraisal. This time, their home was valued at $1.48 million.[33]

They took legal action and reached a settlement that

included not just monetary compensation but also a requirement for the appraiser to attend antidiscrimination training and watch a documentary on appraisal bias. "Having to erase our identity to get a better appraisal was a wrenching experience," Tate-Austin said. "We want others to know that if you experience discrimination, you can fight back."[34]

Their stories are not isolated. A 2021 study by Freddie Mac found that homes in Black neighborhoods are more than twice as likely to be undervalued compared to similar homes in white neighborhoods.[35] And a 2018 Brookings Institution report estimates that this widespread devaluation has cost Black homeowners $156 billion in lost equity.[36]

Those historical choices are not just archived in legislation—they're etched into the geography of our cities and the location of our sanctuaries. Even today, many churches that once benefited from discriminatory housing policies remain planted in well-resourced communities. They host food drives and organize mission trips but often remain disconnected from the structural forces that created the disparities they now seek to address.

You and I both know this isn't just about history. When we talk about the church's role in economic injustice, we're also talking about the churches that welcomed our white neighbors while redlining boxed our families out. We're talking about sermons that preached personal holiness but stayed silent on generational harm.

This isn't about condemning anyone. But it *is* about naming truth. Because the gospel is big enough to hold both grace and accountability—but grace without truth is just avoidance. If we're serious about justice, we can't keep settling for charity while dodging the deeper work of repair. We can't celebrate generosity from churches that have never grappled with how inequality was designed—and how often the church helped reinforce it.

This isn't about guilt. It's about responsibility. About what it really means to follow Jesus in a world shaped by injustice. And whether those who claim his name are willing to follow him into the hard, humbling work of repair.

The New Jim Crow

I didn't grow up visiting prisons. I didn't have close friends or family members who were incarcerated when I was young. But when I first started reading about mass incarceration—really reading about it—I couldn't shake what I was learning.

It was Michelle Alexander's *The New Jim Crow: Mass Incarceration in the Age of Colorblindness* that turned the lights on for me. I remember sitting with the book open and feeling a slow burn in my chest as she laid out the connections between slavery, Jim Crow, and the so-called War on Drugs. She wasn't just naming injustice—she was exposing a system that had been hiding in plain sight. In the decades following the Civil Rights Movement, America began building what Alexander calls "the new Jim Crow"—a racialized system of social control that replaced old forms of segregation with a new one: prison. I had heard the statistics. I'd seen the headlines. But this was different. This was history reframed. It was policy and theology colliding.

One line in particular gripped me: "We have not ended racial caste in America; we have merely redesigned it."[37] That sentence lodged itself in my mind. I couldn't stop thinking about the young men who used to pack the front row of youth services—and how, over time, those rows emptied out. I thought about families in my community carrying a quiet pain they rarely named. I thought about how easy it is for churches to focus on personal sin while ignoring the systems that target and trap our people generation after generation.

That book didn't just give me knowledge—it gave me grief. And that grief became conviction. Because if prison has become one of the most consistent institutions in Black communities, replacing the pulpit, the schoolhouse, and the neighborhood center, then preaching can't stay abstract. Our theology has to speak to the chains we see now—not just the ones our ancestors wore.

I didn't have to be behind bars or know someone who was to recognize the weight of this system. I just had to listen. And once I did, I couldn't preach the same way again.

This is why our ministry at the church intentionally focuses on families and the children in our community. We've structured everything to meet practical needs—starting with education. Each year, we award nearly $300,000 in college scholarships. We operate a counseling center that offers professional care from licensed therapists and psychologists, because we believe mental health is sacred too. Our youth programs are designed not only to keep boys and girls off the streets but to cultivate their gifts—to show them they matter and they belong. We support families through health and wellness initiatives, because thriving isn't just spiritual—it's physical, emotional, and communal.

Now, we're only one church. I know I can't help *everyone*. But I *can* help *someone*—one child at a time, one family at a time. That's my commitment. That's my calling. I believe it's my duty, as a spiritual leader in my community, to make sure our people are growing holistically—in mind, body, and spirit. My prayer is that, by doing so, we can keep them out of a system designed to derail their future. From the streets to the structures, we're fighting for their freedom every single day.

This isn't just ministry. It's resistance. Because when you know that the system is stacked against your people, you don't just preach hope, you build lifelines. You disrupt the cycle. You stand in the gap before they fall through. That's why we fight so hard for our youth—because we know what's waiting if we don't.

If redlining shaped where people could live, mass incarceration determined whether they could live free. And as with redlining, it was never just about crime—it was about control.

The transformation began in the 1970s when President Richard Nixon launched the so-called War on Drugs. His domestic policy adviser, John Ehrlichman, later admitted in a 1994 interview, "We knew we couldn't make it illegal to be either against the war or Black . . . but by getting the public to associate the hippies with marijuana and Blacks with heroin, and then criminalizing both heavily, we could disrupt those communities."[38]

By the 1980s, the Reagan administration escalated this war with the Anti-Drug Abuse Act of 1986, introducing mandatory minimum sentences and a staggering 100:1 sentencing disparity between crack cocaine, more prevalent in Black neighborhoods, and powder cocaine, more commonly used by white Americans.[39]

The consequences were devastating. In 1980 about three hundred thousand people were incarcerated in the United States. By 2021 that number had ballooned to more than 1.2 million people in prison alone, with an additional 636,300 in jails, bringing the total incarcerated population to nearly 1.9 million.[40] In 2022, Black Americans were incarcerated at a rate of 1,196 per 100,000 adults compared to 229 per 100,000 for white Americans, a ratio of more than five to one.[41] A 2003 federal report estimated that one in three Black boys born that year would be incarcerated at some point in their lives if trends continued.[42]

But it wasn't just about time behind bars. Mass incarceration fractured families, stripped voting rights, and created lifelong barriers to housing, employment, and education. The prison system became a pipeline—one that shaped entire communities around absence and stigma.

And the church? With some exceptions, it mostly watched from the sidelines.

Many white churches interpreted the rise in incarceration as a crisis of personal morality rather than of structural injustice. Instead of asking why Black men were being disproportionately targeted and imprisoned, they preached sermons on personal responsibility. They offered forgiveness—but not reform. Prayer—but not policy change. As historian Aaron Griffith notes, white evangelicals in particular "championed personal redemption but often failed to challenge the punitive policies that devastated communities of color."[43]

This theology aligned comfortably with "tough on crime" rhetoric. Instead of seeing mass incarceration as a racialized system of control, many Christian leaders interpreted it as a reflection of moral decay. They offered compassion for prisoners while voting for the policies that put them there. As Griffith writes, "Evangelicals largely accepted punitive views of criminal justice, celebrating police and law-and-order politicians and offering spiritual explanations for crime that ignored structural realities."[44]

Some churches actively supported the political efforts that expanded the prison system and made mass incarceration a way of life. They endorsed "law and order" candidates, used theological language to justify harsh sentencing, and lent moral legitimacy to policies that disproportionately targeted Black communities. Their theology addressed personal sin but had little to say about the systems that perpetuated harm.

Other churches didn't speak out at all. Their silence wasn't neutral—it was costly. It meant fewer prophetic voices calling out injustice. It meant more children growing up without parents. It meant entire neighborhoods devastated, even as pulpits preached messages about "order" and "respectability."

Whether through active endorsement or quiet omission, the result was the same: The church helped normalize a system that prioritized punishment over restoration—and control over justice.

The consequences of mass incarceration persist today in systems that continue to punish poverty and entrench racial inequity. Cash bail systems, for instance, routinely detain people simply because they can't afford to pay. As a 2019 report from the Center for American Progress explained, "In effect, the cash bail system criminalizes poverty, as people who are unable to afford bail are detained while they await trial for weeks or even months. Cash bail perpetuates inequities in the justice system that are disproportionately felt by communities of color and those experiencing poverty."[45]

Probation and parole structures also reinforce inequality. According to the ACLU and Human Rights Watch, "Probation and parole often set people up to fail—with arbitrary rules, burdensome fees, and the constant threat of re-incarceration for non-criminal violations."[46] And in many neighborhoods the reality of over-policing remains unchanged. The Sentencing Project notes that "Black Americans are more likely to be arrested, convicted, and sentenced more harshly than their white counterparts—even when charged with the same offenses," and that this is particularly true in "communities that are both over-policed and under-resourced."[47]

These aren't relics of the past. They're the present reality—lived daily by millions of Americans.

So the question becomes this: If the church preaches liberty, does it include *my* freedom? If it talks about grace, does it extend that grace to *my* people? If it calls for justice, does it mean justice for *me*—or just for those already in power?

Because if the gospel we're hearing makes room for individual repentance but has no space for collective repair, then we haven't just missed the point—we've built a theology that knows how to look away when it's *we* who are hurting.

And, far too often, that theology hasn't just looked away—it's fused itself with power. It's baptized nationalism, cloaked injustice in patriotism, and preached a version of faith more loyal to the flag than to the cross. That's when Christianity stops being good news for the oppressed and becomes a tool for maintaining control.

When Christianity Gets Wrapped in a Flag

I remember the moment it hit me that something was deeply off. It wasn't during a Sunday service or a national holiday—it was in a string of Zoom meetings and email threads with fellow pastors. These were white evangelical leaders I had once shared pulpits with, prayed with, and called brothers in Christ. But as the 2020 election drew near, something shifted.

They didn't just say they were voting Republican. They insisted *real* Christians had no other choice. One email even said, "If you're not voting Republican, I don't know how you can claim to follow Jesus." In one breath, they equated party loyalty with discipleship—and in doing so exposed a theology that had traded the kingdom for a campaign.

I sat there grieving because I realized how far we had drifted from the gospel. The Jesus I follow isn't red or blue. He's not beholden to ballots or national borders. He didn't die for a platform. He died for people. And yet here were leaders tying salvation itself to a party line.

That moment changed how I preach. It made me more careful with my language and more courageous with my convictions. Because if we don't name the difference between Christ and Christian nationalism, we'll end up preaching a gospel that saves no one and protects only power.

I've spent years preaching the gospel. But lately I've found myself asking, "*Which* gospel are we preaching?"

Because there's a version of Christianity being proclaimed in this country that sounds less like the teachings of Jesus of Nazareth and more like a civil religion draped in red, white, and blue. It wraps a flag around the cross and calls it faith. But what it offers isn't salvation—it's supremacy.

White Christian nationalism isn't just a political ideology—it's a theological distortion. It fuses allegiance to Christ with allegiance to country—and, too often, with allegiance to whiteness. It presents America as God's uniquely chosen nation and treats any challenge as disloyalty, not just to the country, but to God himself. That's not just misguided. It's idolatry.

Sociologists Andrew Whitehead and Samuel Perry define Christian nationalism as a framework built on myths, traditions, and narratives of America's founding as a Christian nation—one ordained by God, endowed with power and wealth, destined to be a shining example to the world. Their work shows that these mythic ideas still shape public identity and policy.[48] They shape how people vote, how they think about race, and how they interpret Scripture.

We saw it in full color on January 6, 2021. Rioters stormed the US Capitol waving "Jesus Saves" banners alongside Confederate flags. Some carried wooden crosses. Others raised signs that read "Trump Is My President" and "Jesus 2020" as they pushed past barricades. On the Capitol lawn, they erected a large cross while chanting "Hang Mike Pence." That wasn't a contradiction. It was a collision—between Christian symbolism and white-supremacist violence. And it didn't happen overnight. It was taught—discipled over years. Sometimes from pulpits. Sometimes in Bible studies. Often in silence.

Groups like the Jericho March show just how deeply this theology has taken root. They described their rallies as "peaceful prayer walks," but what they were really doing was reenacting biblical warfare imagery to justify overturning an election. Shofars. Worship music. Prophetic declarations. They marched around government buildings not to call for justice—but to demand power.

This is what happens when Christianity is hijacked by nationalism. It's not just a theological misstep. It's a spiritual crisis.

And while some pastors tried to distance themselves from what happened, far too many stayed quiet. Others spiritualized it, claiming "we shouldn't be political." But silence in the face of Christian nationalism isn't neutrality. It's complicity.

I've seen it firsthand. Pastors who wouldn't name white supremacy for fear of offending tithing members. Congregants who were taught that being a good Christian meant voting a certain way, supporting endless wars, or defending policies that harmed people who look like us. That's not discipleship. That's indoctrination.

What makes this so dangerous is how easily it uses Scripture to sanctify empire. Verses meant to point to God's kingdom get twisted to bless American exceptionalism. Take 2 Chronicles 7:14—"If my people, who are called by my name . . ." You've probably seen it on bumper stickers or National Day of Prayer banners. But that promise wasn't made to the United States. It was made to ancient Israel. And using the Bible as a blueprint for American revival turns scriptures into political slogans and treats the United States like God's covenant nation.

That's not just bad theology. It's dangerous theology. Because it shifts our hope away from the kingdom of God and attaches it to the success of a nation-state. It confuses patriotism with faith. It swaps Jesus' mission for a political agenda.

But here's the truth: America is not the church. And the church is not a voting bloc.

Jesus didn't die for a flag. He died to reconcile all things to himself. When faith gets fused with nationalism, we trade the cross for a sword. We replace humility with dominance. Grace with entitlement.

And we've seen this story before.

In the Gospels, many people expected a messiah who would lead a revolution—someone who would overthrow Rome and reestablish Israel's national power. They weren't looking for a Savior. They were looking for a strongman. A political fixer. A cultural warrior. But Jesus didn't come waving a flag. He came washing feet.

He preached enemy love instead of revenge. He chose the cross over conquest. And because he didn't meet their nationalist expectations, they rejected him.

That temptation is alive and well today.

When our theology becomes tethered to national identity—when we expect God's kingdom to show up through legislation, elections, and cultural dominance—we make the same mistake. We want a Jesus who secures our side's power, not one who sacrifices himself for everyone, including his opposers. But Jesus is not the mascot of any empire. He is the crucified Lamb.

And white Christian nationalism is a modern messianic misfire. It confuses cultural dominance with spiritual authority. It co-opts Christian language while rejecting Christ's actual mission.

And the consequences aren't just theological. They're racial.

Research shows that white Christian nationalism correlates with higher racial resentment, stronger anti-immigrant views, and deeper opposition to justice efforts. Those who embrace Christian nationalism are more likely to deny systemic racism and oppose any policy that seeks to repair its harm.

That's not an accident.

When Christianity is used to justify power instead of justice, it stops sounding like good news to people on the margins. It stops looking like Jesus.

So here's the question I need the church to ask—especially the church in this country: Who are we really following? Are we shaped by the Sermon on the Mount or by Manifest Destiny? Are we disciples of the crucified Savior or defenders of a cultural tribe? Do we carry the cross—or just wear it as jewelry while waving the flag?

Because once our faith gets fused with the pursuit of dominance, we stop following Jesus and start following something else.

Loving your country isn't the problem. But when nationalism replaces the gospel—or hijacks it—we lose our witness. We trade the humility of the cross for the hunger for control. And if this version of the gospel doesn't have room for justice—if it doesn't affirm the dignity of the oppressed, or speak the truth about racial harm—then I understand why so many of us are walking away. Not from Jesus. But from the institutions that keep using his name to baptize their own power.

The Jesus I follow doesn't call us to protect our privilege. He calls us to lay it down.

He doesn't ask us to win political wars. He invites us to love sacrificially—even when it costs us something.

So let's be clear: Christian nationalism is not the gospel. It never was. When white supremacy drapes itself in Scripture and calls itself Christianity, it's still what it's always been—a lie.

And what's wild? Some of the same folks who label Black liberation theology as "too political" have no problem turning churches into campaign headquarters. Nationalism is only a problem when it's not theirs.

If we can't call out that double standard—if we can't name these distortions with clarity and love—then we've got work to do. Not just in our theology but in our integrity.

Because this isn't just about bad ideas. It's about broken witness.

The gospel is too precious, and the harm too real, for anything less than the full truth.

Reckoning with What's Already Happened

Though my roots are deeply embedded in the Black church and community, much of my professional journey has unfolded in predominantly white churches and Christian institutions. In those spaces, I've built lasting relationships and seen glimpses of what the kingdom could be. But when the topic turned to justice, something shifted. The air would change. Conversations stalled. Eyes looked away. The silence didn't feel like reflection—it felt like avoidance.

I've sat in meetings where people prayed for unity while refusing to acknowledge inequality. I've heard pastors talk about wanting a diverse church but making no meaningful changes to create one. They would profess love for the Black community, yet remain silent from the pulpit when injustice screamed from the headlines. And more than once I've been in rooms where someone casually declared, "Social justice isn't biblical"—as if the call to do justice, love mercy, and walk humbly with God was somehow disconnected from how we treat the oppressed.

That kind of silence isn't neutral. It's a decision. And that phrase—"Social justice isn't biblical"? That's not just a theological stance. It's a refusal to act. A subtle but powerful way of blessing the status quo.

I'm not the only one who has felt that tension. Barna's 2021 Trends in the Black Church study found that nearly three in ten Black practicing Christians who attend multiracial congregations report experiencing racial prejudice.[49] And many Black young adults have grown cynical about the church's credibility because of its inadequate response to racial injustice.[50] I've lived that. I've sat in rooms where I had to translate my pain into language that seemed palatable.

But let me be clear: Hope isn't the same as denial. I don't believe the church is beyond healing, but I do believe it needs to be honest about the harm. Because what you and I have seen—the hypocrisy, the half-truths, the selective silence—is real. And it's one of the reasons so many of our brothers and sisters are walking away.

Not from Jesus. But from churches that no longer reflect him.

Recent surveys from Pew confirm that while most

Americans agree that racism is a problem, we are deeply divided over what to do about it. Nearly six in ten Black adults say US laws and institutions need to be completely rebuilt because they are fundamentally biased. Only 18 percent of white adults agree. The gap isn't just political. It's theological. We're not starting from the same understanding of the problem—and that makes moving forward incredibly difficult.

So before we talk about solutions, we need to name the wound.

When you've been ignored, dismissed, or spiritually gaslit in the name of "unity," it's not apathy to walk away—it's exhaustion. For many Black Christians, the exit isn't a rejection of Christ. It's a rejection of what the church has become.

That's where we end this chapter. Not with an altar call. But with an honest reckoning.

Because if the church can't tell the truth about itself, why should you trust it to tell the truth about God?

THREE

Black Americans Are Leaving Church

I DIDN'T HEAR IT FROM A STRANGER. I heard it from family.

My sister and my sister-in-law—both faithful, both prayerful, both deeply rooted in the church—each made the same painful decision, just months apart. They had to step away. Not because they stopped believing in Jesus, but because they couldn't keep pretending everything was okay in a place that refused to see them.

What broke them wasn't a dramatic moment of betrayal. It was the slow erosion that comes when your pain is ignored week after week. When injustice roars in the streets but never gets a mention in the sanctuary. When your pastor preaches passionately about "truth" and "righteousness" but never once says the names of the people dying unjustly in your community. When the gospel becomes less about the cross and more about a candidate.

And, in both cases, their pastors were white men—leaders they had respected, listened to, and prayed for. That made the silence even louder. Because when the pulpit speaks boldly about everything *except* the lives of people who look like you, the message is clear—even if no one says it out loud.

Both of them told me, separately, that it stopped feeling like church. One said, "It's not about Jesus anymore. It's about their political party." The other said, "If my life doesn't matter enough to even be prayed about, why am I still sitting here?"

Their words sat heavy with me. Because I knew they weren't walking away out of bitterness. They were walking away because they had stayed as long as they could. They had hoped for more—for truth, for courage, for someone to stand in the pulpit and name what was happening. But instead they were met with silence. And that silence became a wall.

I've heard people say Black folks are leaving the church because they're angry. But that's not what I've seen. What I've seen is grief. A quiet heartbreak that builds when the church that taught you to follow Jesus forgets how to walk like him.

They didn't lose faith. They lost trust.

And when trust breaks, everything shifts.

Some of the hardest conversations I've had as a pastor haven't been with people who've lost their faith—they've been with people who still want to believe but no longer know how to do it in church. People who still love Jesus but can't stomach the silence they've encountered—especially in white churches that stayed quiet while injustice roared. People who grew up in pews, sang in choirs, recited memory verses, and gave their all to the life of the church—but now sit outside the sanctuary asking, *Is there still a place for me?*

Because that silence—the silence around racism, around Black suffering, around the church's own complicity—isn't neutral. It wounds. And for many Black Christians, especially in white-majority spaces, the weight of that betrayal has become too much to carry. The grief is deep. The frustration is real. And so more and more are walking away.

Some have called it "the Black exodus." Others, "the quiet exodus." But for those living it, it feels like heartbreak.

And it's not just about leaving a particular church or denomination. It's about a deeper reckoning: How can Christianity offer redemption when it's been so entangled with racial injustice? For younger generations in particular, it's getting harder and harder to reconcile faith in Jesus with the institutions that claimed his name but refused to stand up for his people.

That dissonance runs deep. It's layered with generational pain—stories handed down through hushed conversations, glances across pews, unspoken rules of survival. And when churches won't hold space for that pain, when they brush it aside or label it "divisive," people don't always fight back. They just leave.

And yet, even in that disillusionment, the Black church remains one of the few spaces where the gospel has consistently been proclaimed—not as control but as liberation. Where faith wasn't limited to the pulpit but lived out in protest marches, in hospital visits, in choir stands and Communion tables, in kitchens and courtrooms. It has carried our people through storms we were never meant to survive.

The Black church has not been perfect. But it has been faithful. And for those still wrestling with what to believe and where to belong, that legacy still offers credibility—a witness to a gospel that liberates, restores, and tells the truth.

Losing Trust, Leaving Church

For many of us, the Black church remains a sacred space where the gospel has meant redemption and liberation, not control. That legacy still speaks.

Nevertheless, more and more Black Americans are stepping away from Christianity.

And that tension—that even a liberating church tradition hasn't been enough to stem the tide of disaffiliation—should cause us to pause. According to Pew, more than one-third of Black adults now identify as having no religious affiliation—what some call the "nones." And this shift isn't just notable; it's historic.

In 2008, African Americans were the least likely of all racial groups to be unaffiliated with any religion—just 19.5 percent identified as nones. At the time, Black religious life was widely recognized as one of the most devout and institutionally rooted in the country. But by 2020 that had changed. The number of Black Americans with no religious affiliation had surged to 34.9 percent, surpassing both white (30.1 percent) and Hispanic (23 percent) respondents. Over just twelve years, that fifteen-point jump was the most dramatic shift among any group.

That kind of movement doesn't happen by accident. And it should get our attention.

It's especially striking when you consider the centrality of faith in Black life across generations. Through slavery, Jim Crow, segregation, and structural racism, Black communities clung to faith as a lifeline. As historian Albert Raboteau has written, "The spirituals, sermons, and testimony meetings of the slave religion not only sustained hope for eventual deliverance but created a sense of identity and moral agency in a world that denied both."[1]

So what has changed?

Credibility.

Young Black adults, especially millennials and Gen Z, are no longer willing to compartmentalize their spiritual beliefs from their experience of injustice. They are asking questions the church too often avoids: If the church won't speak out against racial injustice, how can it claim to follow Jesus? When pastors stay silent about police violence—or, worse, defend it—people don't just leave churches. They walk away from the version of Christianity that allowed such silence to seem holy.

As Lisa Fields, founder of the Jude 3 Project, has observed, many young Black Christians are asking deep theological questions—about race, justice, identity—and finding that some churches don't offer spaces safe enough to wrestle with those questions. She's heard stories of people who leave not because they've lost faith but because they're looking for a faith that can reflect their full story.[2]

A 2022 article in *Christianity Today* reflects what many of us are hearing in our own communities. Sociologist and pastor Ryan Burge writes, "Black Americans are leaving church at a faster clip than any other demographic. The reasons are many—but a recurring theme is disillusionment with religious institutions that appear indifferent to their lived realities."[3]

This disaffection isn't about style. It's about substance. It's about a church that chooses civility over truth, political alliances over prophetic witness, and comfort over the cross.

And when the church reflects the priorities of the powerful more than the values of the kingdom, people take notice. They walk away.

Not Leaving Jesus, Just What's Been Done in His Name

The reasons so many Black Americans are leaving the church aren't simple—but they're not a mystery either. This exodus didn't come out of nowhere, as the previous chapters have shown. It's a response to a long and painful history in which Christianity in America has too often failed to reflect the heart of Christ—especially for Black believers.

Many of us were raised hearing the gospel of salvation, redemption, and radical oneness in Christ. We memorized verses about freedom, grace, and love. We were told that in Christ there is no Jew or gentile, slave or free, male or female. But as we grew older, many of us began to see the gap between what was preached and what was practiced. We saw churches that spoke about unity but stayed segregated. We heard sermons about forgiveness but silence about injustice. We were taught that Jesus sets the captives free, but the institutions bearing his name often upheld the very chains he came to break.

It wasn't just disappointing. It was disorienting.

Because the message of Jesus still resonates. The vision of salvation and healing, of community and liberation—that still moves people. But what's been done in his name? That's what people are walking away from. They're not rejecting the truth. They're rejecting the distortion.

Unhealed History

For many Black Christians, the church's failure isn't news—it's a wound we've traced before. The history has been named: how the same Bible that speaks of justice was once used to justify slavery, how churches that now preach unity once defended segregation. But knowing that history isn't the same as being free from its impact.

Because that memory doesn't just live in the past—it lives in the body. It shows up in the tension we carry walking into a church that's never acknowledged what it once endorsed. It lingers in the skepticism we feel when the word *justice* is treated like a distraction from the gospel. And in the absence of confession or repair, that memory doesn't fade. It festers.

Scholar and public theologian Willie James Jennings describes this legacy as a "diseased social imagination"[4]—a version of Christianity distorted to serve conquest, whiteness, and exclusion rather than the liberating purposes of Christ. When churches refuse to reckon with that legacy, it's not just history they're ignoring—it's people. People who are still in the pews. Still on the margins. Still trying to breathe under the weight of a gospel they were taught to love but rarely saw lived out.

It's hard to trust institutions that still won't say the word *racism* out loud. Hard to feel at home in sanctuaries that welcome our tithes but not our testimony. Hard to believe in repentance when there's never been accountability.

Silence = "You Don't Matter"

During the Civil Rights Movement, most white churches didn't just stay out of the fight—they resisted it. They talked about staying "neutral" or keeping politics out of the pulpit, but that so-called neutrality always seemed to fall on the side of the status quo. Dr. King saw it for what it was. In his "Letter from Birmingham Jail," he said he was more disappointed with the white moderate than with outright opponents of justice. Why? Because the moderate preferred "a negative peace which is the absence of tension to a positive peace which is the presence of justice."[5]

That same kind of silence showed up again during the

COVID-19 pandemic and the national outcry that followed the murders of George Floyd, Breonna Taylor, and Ahmaud Arbery. But this time, Black Christians weren't staying quiet. We filled the streets—not to push a political agenda but to declare a spiritual truth: that our lives, our pain, and our dignity matter to God, and should matter to the church.

And yet, even then, in many churches—especially in multiracial or white-majority spaces—those cries were met with awkward silences, vague calls for unity, or shallow sermons that skipped right over repentance. It didn't feel like support. It felt like distance. Like dismissal. Like doors quietly closing behind us.

Meanwhile, Black communities were carrying a different kind of grief.

We were hit hard by the pandemic—not just financially, but physically. Our families were nearly three times as likely to be hospitalized or die from COVID-19. These weren't statistics. These were our elders. Our neighbors. Our loved ones. And while we were burying family members and trying to keep kids in school without reliable Wi-Fi or enough devices, many of the churches that had the most resources said the least.

I remember how our church in Inglewood responded. We didn't have a grant or a formal program, but we had people in need. So we bought laptops. We installed hot spots. We made space for kids to learn. Because the need was urgent, and we couldn't look away.

But we also couldn't ignore who *did* look away.

The silence wasn't just institutional. It felt personal.

When churches with big budgets and empty buildings did nothing, the message was clear: You're on your own.

And when silence becomes the norm, it stops feeling like a communication breakdown. It starts to feel like abandonment.

That's the real weight many young Black believers carry. We grew up hearing "we're all one in Christ." But we've watched how that unity breaks down when it's time to confront racism. We've watched love get quiet when justice is on the line. And when your grief isn't acknowledged, your story isn't welcomed, and your humanity isn't affirmed, you begin to ask, *Do I even belong here?*

As Anthea Butler argues in *White Evangelical Racism*, Black Christians often share theological beliefs with white evangelicals, yet still find themselves ignored, dismissed, or overlooked when they raise concerns about racial justice.[6]

That kind of dismissal doesn't just hurt—it drives people out. And if no one names it, the exit looks like apathy. But it's not apathy. It's heartbreak.

That's why some of us have stopped showing up. Not because we've given up on Jesus, but because we're tired of being in places that act like we don't matter.

When Power Replaces Compassion

The Black exodus isn't just about what churches have failed to say—it's also about the alliances they've chosen to make.

Over the past several years, many Black Christians have

watched white churches grow increasingly aligned with political movements that don't just misunderstand us—they actively work against our dignity. These churches didn't just ignore racial injustice. They linked arms with candidates and platforms that denied it even existed.

We saw it when churches praised "law and order" rhetoric while our communities were pleading for police accountability. When voting rights were stripped away through restrictive laws in Georgia, Texas, and Florida, many churches said nothing—or backed the politicians behind the bills. We saw outrage over protests but not over the murders that caused them. We heard pulpits condemn critical race theory but say nothing about the school-to-prison pipeline or racial wealth gap. And when immigrant families were torn apart at the border, some church leaders quoted Romans 13 to justify it.

This alignment wasn't just political. It felt spiritual. It sent a message about whose suffering mattered—and whose didn't.

When churches defend systems that harm the vulnerable. When they speak more loudly about tax policies than police killings. When they care more about protecting cultural dominance than lifting up the poor and the hurting. You start to ask the question plainly: Whose side is the church really on?

The Jesus we were raised to love didn't sidestep injustice. He touched the leper. He flipped the tables. He walked with the excluded. He stood with the poor and called out the powerful. But somewhere along the way too many churches stopped following that Jesus. They stopped centering compassion and started chasing control. The gospel got co-opted by political agendas. The pulpit became a platform for preserving influence.

And that shift hasn't gone unnoticed.

As a Black pastor, I've felt it personally. The church feels politically distant and spiritually adrift. I still believe in the power of the gospel, but I've had to wrestle with what it means to proclaim that gospel in places where it's been weaponized. Because when sermons sound more like stump speeches, when prayer meetings sound like campaign rallies, when your pain is treated as a threat to "unity," it becomes harder and harder to recognize Jesus in the house that claims his name.

And if that's what you've seen—if you've watched the church choose power over people—it makes sense that you'd start to pull away.

Why White Christian Nationalism Confirms the Exit

You've probably felt it too—that growing sense that something in the church just doesn't line up anymore. It's not that you stopped believing in Jesus. It's that the version of Christianity you're seeing in this country feels more like politics than power from on high. And for many of us it's become the final straw.

White Christian nationalism has been gaining steam—and we've seen what it does. It takes the gospel and remixes it into something else: a flag-waving, power-chasing faith that's more about dominance than deliverance. It merges belief in

Jesus with a narrow, whitewashed vision of American identity. It equates cultural control with God's will and treats anyone outside that vision as suspect.

This isn't just coming from the margins. It's gone mainstream—especially in white evangelical spaces.

A 2023 study found that nearly two-thirds of white evangelical Protestants are either Christian-nationalism adherents or sympathizers.[7] That's not a fringe group. It's a majority within the most prominent theological bloc in American Protestantism.

Even more sobering: Among those identified as Christian nationalists—who make up 29 percent of the US population—two-thirds identify as white evangelicals.[8]

So when you hear someone, say "God has called Christians to exercise dominion over all areas of American society," that's not a random voice on the margins. It represents a movement that's both theologically influential and politically emboldened. And if you're Black in America, you already know what dominion has looked like. We've lived it. And it never included us.

When that kind of theology shows up in the pulpit, it doesn't feel like conviction—it feels like a warning. When sermons sound more like campaign speeches. When biblical justice is waved off as "wokeness." When pastors defend platforms of power while ignoring the cries of the oppressed. It becomes painfully clear: You're not really part of the vision.

Let's be real—white Christian nationalism didn't start the Black exodus. We've been seeing the cracks for a long time. But it confirmed what many of us already suspected:

that too many churches are more invested in protecting their privilege than practicing the gospel.

So if you've been feeling as if you're on the outside, as if your story doesn't fit in the version of Christianity that's being preached, you're not crazy. You're paying attention.

Losing the Gospel in the Voting Booth

Let's be honest: It's not just Christian nationalism that's pushing people out—it's the way churches have let faith itself get swallowed up by politics. When Christianity starts sounding more like a political-party platform than the teachings of Jesus, it's natural to ask, "Is this really what we signed up for?"

The 2024 election made that disconnect even harder to ignore. Seeing Donald Trump return to the national stage—and watching how many white churches still rallied around him—was jarring. Here was a man whose words and policies around race, policing, and immigration felt like a slap in the face to communities like ours. And yet some churches didn't just stay quiet. They offered their full-throated support.

And that silence? It didn't feel like neutrality. It felt like betrayal.

For many of us, it was a moment of spiritual disillusionment. A moment when we realized that some churches cared more about being close to political power than being close to the people who are hurting. That hurt deepened when anti-immigrant rhetoric, hostility toward the poor, and policies rooted in fear started showing up not just on news channels but in sermons.

What made it worse wasn't just who they voted for. It was

how they treated anyone who disagreed. Suddenly, if you questioned the morality of that support, your faith was suspect. If you saw justice and compassion as central to the gospel, your loyalty to Christ was doubted. If you raised your voice in grief or concern, you were seen as divisive—or ungrateful.

And for many of us the impact wasn't just emotional—it was personal. Communities of color felt the weight of these decisions. Immigrant families began to worry whether showing up to church would make them vulnerable to ICE raids. When the Trump administration floated removing protections for churches and schools as "sensitive locations," it sent a clear message: Even the sanctuary might not be safe anymore. And many churches said nothing. For many of our communities, that silence wasn't just neglect—it was complicity.

Bishop Mark Seitz in El Paso was one of the few who spoke up. He warned that just the perception of immigration enforcement near churches would be enough to keep families away from worship. He was right.

Now, to be clear, we're not pretending these issues are simple. Immigration is complex. So is public spending, national security, and economic stability. There are real tensions here. But if the church won't model what it means to wrestle with those questions in truth and love—if it keeps choosing fear over empathy, slogans over substance—then where else are people supposed to look?

I remember my ethics professor saying, "Voting for the lesser of two evils is still voting for evil." And while we all have to wrestle with the options we're given, what shook me was how quickly some white evangelicals equated loyalty to

Trump with loyalty to Jesus. As if the gospel had a party line. As if their ballot was proof of their salvation—and ours was proof we'd lost our way.

This isn't about pretending any political party has it all right. None of them do. Every policy platform has contradictions. Every leader is flawed. But when the church lets partisanship replace compassion—when it puts access to power ahead of proximity to the poor—it doesn't just lose credibility.

It loses people.

And for many Black Christians, that loss isn't theoretical. It's a wound we're still carrying.

Not Just Leaving White Churches

You already know this: The Black church has never just been about Sunday morning. It's been our sanctuary and our shelter. Our protest and our praise. It held us when nothing else did. Our elders prayed us through the Middle Passage, Reconstruction, Jim Crow, and mass incarceration. Through it all, the Black church kept telling us the truth: You are made in God's image. You are not what this country tried to make you believe.

We sang our survival. We preached our hope. And, somehow, that faith carried us.

But even in our own spaces, something's shifting.

More and more Black Christians—especially young ones—aren't just leaving white churches. They're walking away from church altogether. And it's not because they've stopped believing in God. Most still pray. Many still love Jesus. But they're tired of the disconnect. Tired of hearing about a God of justice while watching churches dodge real conversations about inequality. Tired of being told to calm down, tone it down, or leave parts of themselves at the door just to belong.

There's a growing question bubbling up: Do I have to choose between being fully Black and fully Christian?

That question isn't coming from a place of rebellion. It's coming from disappointment. From fatigue. From trying to worship in places that never make space for your grief. From hearing messages about "kingdom identity" while your actual identity is treated like a threat.

And now even the Black church has to wrestle. Are we still a refuge for the wounded, or have we become so polished that we've forgotten the power in being raw and real? Are we doing the work of liberation—or just protecting the institutions we've built?

These aren't questions of abandonment. They're questions of survival.

If we're going to reach and keep the next generation, we've got to make room for their honesty—their doubts, their anger, their hunger for something deeper than church as usual. We've got to be the kind of church where performance gives way to presence. Where pain has a place. Where faith isn't just inherited—it's lived.

Because they're not asking for entertainment. They're asking for truth. And they're watching to see whether the church they were raised in is ready to tell it.

The Question That Won't Let Us Go

If you've ever sat with the question "How can I be Black and Christian?" you're not alone.

You might not have said it out loud. But maybe you've felt it. Especially when history won't let you forget what's been done in Jesus' name. Especially when you've been asked to forgive without justice. When churches told you your life mattered to God—but then said nothing when that life was threatened in the streets. When you kept showing up, hoping to be seen, and left feeling invisible.

For many of us, the question isn't whether we believe in God. We do. It's whether we can still believe in *this* version of Christianity—the one that's been used to colonize, to control, to silence.

This isn't just a theological crisis. It's emotional. It's generational. We inherited faith—but we also inherited pain. And when church becomes a place where there's no room to grieve, no room to ask questions, no space for lament—it stops feeling like home.

That's why ministries such as the Jude 3 Project are so important. Lisa Fields started it to create space for Black Christians to wrestle. Not to pretend. Not to perform. But to bring our whole selves to the table—questions, anger, confusion, all of it. Jude 3 doesn't just defend Christianity from outside critique. It untangles it from the lies that got wrapped around it—especially the lie that whiteness and faith are the same thing.

Because the real problem isn't Jesus. It's the distortion of his message.

What we need isn't another polished defense of the faith. What we need is permission— permission to be honest, to be wounded, to still want Jesus even if we're done with church as usual. What we need is resurrection. And resurrection comes only after you've told the truth about the death.

So if you've been carrying the question "How can I still follow Jesus after everything that's been done in his name?" know this: You're not alone. And the fact that you're still asking means you haven't given up.

"That's the White Man's Religion"

If you've spent time in our community—especially among those who've stepped away from church—you've probably heard the phrase "Christianity is the white man's religion."

That's not just a hot take. It's a scar speaking.

For a lot of us, that line holds a story. A memory. A truth that hasn't been fully dealt with.

We know what slavery did. We know what colonialism did. We know how often Christianity was introduced, not to set us free, but to keep us in line. White missionaries brought Bibles in one hand and power in the other. On plantations, the same gospel that promised liberation was twisted into chains. After emancipation, the church didn't heal the divide—it reinforced it. We were segregated in the pews, excluded from leadership, told to be quiet and wait for heaven while others built their kingdoms on earth.

That history doesn't fade. It lingers in the background whenever someone preaches unity but won't say the word *justice*. It echoes when churches downplay racism or treat inequality as though it's just the result of a lack of effort. And it confirms what so many already suspect: that Christianity was never really *for us*—just *used on us*.

That's the spiritual dissonance so many of us feel. How can a faith once used to oppress our people now be trusted to liberate them? When no one's making space for that question, walking away starts to feel like the only honest response.

But let's be clear: That version of Christianity—the one rooted in empire, control, and silence—is not the gospel. It never was.

The Jesus who walked the dusty roads of Galilee didn't come for the powerful. He came for the poor. He stood with the marginalized. He flipped the tables and disrupted the systems. He didn't defend the status quo—he broke it open. The real tragedy isn't just what's been done in his name. It's how many people never got the chance to meet him for who he truly is.

So if you've ever wondered whether this faith can still be yours—whether it can hold your Blackness, your questions, your rage, your hope—the answer is yes. Not because of the version that's been weaponized, but because of the one that still sets people free.

When Trust Breaks, Everything Shifts

When trust breaks in the church, the impact doesn't stay in one place. It spreads. It settles deep. It reshapes how we see God, how we see one another, and whether we believe there's still a place for us to belong.

For us as Black Christians, that break often carries weight far beyond doctrine. The church was never just a building—it was a lifeline. It was where we found dignity when the world tried to strip it away. It was where our ancestors dared to believe they were beloved by God even while they were shackled by men. So when that sacred space starts to feel unsafe or untrue, it destabilizes something deeper than attendance. It shakes identity. It shatters hope.

We've already walked through some of that betrayal in these opening chapters. We looked at how Scripture itself was distorted—how the Slave Bible literally cut out the hope. How the myth of the curse of Ham was used to make racism seem sacred. We named how, under Jim Crow, churches didn't just stay silent—they actively preached segregation in Jesus' name. And we traced how the silence didn't stop with the end of legal segregation—it echoed into our lifetimes, into our churches, into the moments when we cried out for justice and were met with calls for "unity" that asked us to be quiet.

That kind of distortion leaves scars. And when the wounds go unhealed, trust crumbles.

Leaving church isn't casual. It's not about laziness or apathy. It's often a slow unraveling—marked by grief, disappointment, and the quiet ache of betrayal. Many of us still pray. Still talk to Jesus. Still believe in a God who sees us. But the place that once held our belief no longer feels like it can hold our pain. So we find faith in new places—meditation, music, ancestral practices, solo Scripture study. We keep searching for something sacred that won't demand we split ourselves in two.

And even when belief survives, something still aches. Because there's a kind of strength and solace that comes only through shared worship. Through seeing your grandmother shout "Amen!" and watching your nephew doze off on your lap while the choir sings. That rhythm formed us. When it goes missing, the silence is loud.

What's being lost isn't just a Sunday service—it's a spiritual infrastructure that helped us build a whole way of life. The Black church was never just about religion. It was resistance. It was education. It was economic empowerment and social safety net. It was our news network, our organizing ground, our home base. It held our grief and our joy, our funerals and our revivals. It taught us how to lead and how to love.

So when people leave, they're not just walking away from worship styles or theological stances. They're walking away from something that once held the full weight of Black life. And when that happens, we have to ask: If the church no longer feels like home, how will we carry what it once held? The work still needs doing. The community still needs care. And whether inside or outside the sanctuary, we need new ways to gather, to organize, to pray, to heal.

This moment is not just a moment of departure. It's a demand for something deeper, something more faithful, something more real.

The Black exodus is not just about walking away—it's about refusing to stay silent in places that silenced us. It's about refusing to settle for a version of faith that speaks of grace but is allergic to justice. For those who've left, the question is not whether they still believe in God. It's whether they can believe in *this* version of Christianity. And for those who remain, especially in churches that have benefited from silence, another question arises: Are you willing to tell the truth? Are you ready to be changed?

Because what we're seeing isn't just disillusionment. It's clarity.

We've spent these first chapters naming the bad news: the weaponization of Scripture, the complicity of churches in systems of harm, the silence that stings deeper than words. But it doesn't have to end here.

There's another story to tell.

There are streams within the Christian tradition that many of us were never taught. Voices that were buried. Saints who were silenced. Truths that could've helped us see that the gospel didn't begin on a slave ship and wasn't invented in the West. There is a faith with roots deep in African soil, a faith that resisted empire long before it was co-opted by it.

When I first started discovering that—when I learned that African theologians helped shape Christian doctrine, that Ethiopian Christians were worshiping Jesus before Europe ever heard his name—it did something in me. It didn't erase the pain. But it helped me breathe again. It showed me that the Christianity used to enslave us was not the whole story. That there is something worth reclaiming.

So before we rebuild, we have to recover. Before we move forward, we have to remember who we are.

Because this story we've inherited? It's not over. And the next chapter begins with truth—and with hope.

PART 2

Breaking the Chains

YOU'VE FELT THE WEIGHT OF IT.

You've seen the harm. You've heard the silence. You've wrestled with whether this faith is still worth holding on to. Part 1 was about naming that struggle—about facing the truth that Christianity, as it was handed to us, often came with chains.

But the story doesn't end there.

Even in the darkest chapters, there were glimmers of light—faithful witnesses who refused to let the gospel be reduced to a tool of oppression. This section is about recovering what was buried: the African roots of Christianity, the liberating heart of the gospel, and the long, courageous faith of Black believers who clung to Jesus even when his name was used to harm them.

We'll journey back to ancient Africa, where theologians like Tertullian, Athanasius, and Augustine shaped the foundation of Christian thought—centuries before the gospel reached Europe. We'll remember how that same faith stirred resistance in enslaved people, fueled abolitionists, and empowered prophets such as Harriet Tubman and Fannie Lou Hamer.

In addition, we'll look at the truths that every human bears God's image, that repentance must be real, and that forgiveness without justice isn't healing—it's erasure.

This isn't about acting as though the struggle is over. The scars remain. But even in bondage our people found something real—a Savior who didn't come to preserve empires but to tear them down. A gospel that spoke not just to sin but to systems. A Jesus who still walks with the wounded.

The good news was never born in colonial outposts or revival tents. It was always a liberation story—from Moses standing before Pharaoh to Jesus proclaiming release for the captives. That's the gospel our ancestors carried when every other hope was stripped away. And in their faith we glimpse the gospel as it was always meant to be.

Now it's our turn to remember.

Back to Africa.

If we're going to reclaim what's true and liberating about this faith, we have to start at the roots. But you can't return to something you never knew was there. For many of us, the story of the church begins in Europe, moves through colonization, and ends in disillusionment. But that's not the whole story. In fact, it's not even the beginning.

While Christianity was still forming in Rome, African communities were shaping its theology, building churches, and living out the gospel—centuries before it reached places like Canterbury. African thinkers crafted doctrine. Local traditions nurtured the faith. Indigenous communities passed it down. European missionaries didn't introduce Christianity to Africa—they arrived long after the faith had already taken root and begun to thrive.

One of the most visible symbols of this legacy is the rock-hewn churches of Lalibela in Ethiopia. These sacred structures—carved from solid stone more than nine hundred years ago—bear witness to a level of devotion and ingenuity that continues to inspire. They are the mark not of a borrowed faith but of an African faith lived and loved in context.

This is not just poetic justice—it's historical truth. In his groundbreaking work *How Africa Shaped the Christian Mind*, Thomas Oden argues that Africa served as the formative ground for much of what would later shape Western Christianity. He even titles the opening section of his book "The African Seedbed of Western Christianity," underscoring his conviction that the theological and spiritual foundations of the faith were deeply rooted in African soil—a legacy too often ignored in both the global north and south, leaving many African Christians unaware of the profound inheritance they carry.[1]

He names early African Christian leaders such as Augustine of Hippo, Athanasius of Alexandria, Tertullian, and the martyr Perpetua—not as distant figures from a foreign tradition but as central voices in the story of the Christian church. Their writings helped define doctrines of the Trinity, Christology, and salvation—doctrines still foundational in churches around the world.

Yet when I got to seminary, you would've thought Christianity started in Rome, took a pit stop in Germany with Luther, and then sailed straight to America with the Puritans. Africa barely made it into the story. Not even a sentence or two about Augustine being from North Africa and framing him as a theological giant who shaped global Christianity. No mention of Egypt's central role in early biblical interpretation. No deep dive into Ethiopia's ancient witness. Just a eunuch who was converted.

And I know my experience wasn't unique.

Many seminaries—especially in the West—still treat African Christianity as a footnote, if it's mentioned at all. Colonial narratives and theological bias have narrowed the lens so drastically that entire continents get left in the margins. The global church keeps telling the story of the faith through European eyes, as if that's the only way to see.

But recovering this history means more than adding diversity to a syllabus. It means rewriting the map. It means reclaiming the faith that was always ours.

To reclaim Christianity's liberating power, we have to reclaim the whole story.

Africa at the Heart of Early Christianity

The Christian story I learned and accepted for so long was a westward journey—from Jerusalem to Rome, then to Europe and beyond. But that version leaves out something essential. Before the gospel ever reached European shores, African believers were already part of the story.

One of the first moments that made me realize how deeply I'd been shaped by a Western lens came through a story I had heard my whole life: that of the Ethiopian eunuch in Acts 8. I had always been taught to see this story as an example of the church's growth outward, eventually reaching Europe. But somehow the obvious escaped me. The eunuch was from Ethiopia. An African.

It hit me hard—almost embarrassingly so. One of the very first recorded believers in Jesus in the book of Acts was not just any convert—he was an African official, returning home with the gospel. When he heard the story of Jesus, he didn't hesitate. "Look, here is water," he said to Philip. "What can stand in the way of my being baptized?" (Acts 8:36). His faith was immediate, courageous, and unashamed. And in that moment Africa didn't just show up in the margins of Scripture—it took center stage.

By the second century that presence had deepened. One of the great centers of Christian thought and practice emerged in Alexandria, Egypt. It became a hub of theological development that shaped not only African Christianity but the entire Roman Empire. The famous catechetical school in Alexandria drew some of the brightest Christian minds of the early church—figures such as Clement of Alexandria and Origen. These thinkers wrestled with questions of faith, Scripture, and doctrine in ways that still influence how we understand theology today.

North Africa was one of the earliest powerhouses of the Christian mind and heart. The cities of Alexandria, Carthage, and Hippo formed a kind of intellectual triangle, producing theological insights that rivaled—and, in some cases, predated—the centers of Rome and Constantinople.[2] From Alexandria's catechetical schools to Hippo's pastoral letters, this region gave birth to ideas that still shape the global church.

And not just in North Africa. Farther south, the kingdom of Aksum embraced Christianity as early as the fourth century. When King Ezana declared it the official religion of Ethiopia, the country became one of the first Christian states in the world. The Ethiopian Orthodox Church grew from those early roots, holding fast to its faith even as empires rose and fell around it. To this day, its traditions, music, and theology remain a vibrant and enduring witness.[3]

Yet despite this legacy, many churches and seminaries—especially in the West—rarely teach this part of Christian history. As great as my seminary training was, I don't remember hearing it framed this way. I had to go looking. And what I found shook me—not because it wasn't true, but because I had never been shown it. I learned church history through a European lens. Augustine, for example—I had heard his name countless times, but I honestly thought he was Italian. Nobody ever mentioned that he was African, from what is now Algeria. His skin would have looked more like mine than it appears in the European portraits found in textbooks. The world was different back then, yes—but the absence of Africa in the way we tell the church's story today isn't just an oversight. It's a distortion.

When you erase Africa from the roots of Christianity, you do more than leave out a chapter. You change the shape of the whole story. It gives the impression that our ancestors were outsiders to the faith, when, in fact, they were shaping it. That's not a small detail. It affects how we see God, how we see ourselves, and whether we believe we have a rightful place at the table.

I felt two emotions when I first saw the truth that Africa wasn't a footnote in Christianity's story but one of its early architects—grief and relief. Grief for the years I'd unknowingly carried someone else's version of my faith. Relief because I didn't have to carry it anymore. I could reclaim something deeper—something mine. And I want that for you too. Because this isn't about pride. It's about place. You've always had one.

Meet the African Minds Who Shaped the Faith

Many of us in the Black church grew up hearing deep truths about God's power, the meaning of salvation, and what it looks like to live out the gospel. And if you ever went looking for where those ideas came from, you might've been pointed toward European thinkers. I know I was. Whether it was in the books I read or the way church history was taught, the picture that emerged was overwhelmingly white.

But here's what I wish someone had told me sooner: Some of the most important voices in early Christianity didn't come from Europe. They came from Africa.

Theologians such as Tertullian, Origen, Athanasius, and Augustine weren't just absorbing Christian teachings—they were shaping them. The bold questions they asked about who Jesus was, how salvation worked, what justice meant, and how to live as believers in a broken world continue to be relevant today. These weren't sidebar thinkers.

I must repeat that these heroes of the faith lived and worked in African cities—Alexandria, Carthage, Hippo—bringing an African lens to the growing Christian faith. Too often, they've been cast as European simply because their writings were preserved and promoted by European institutions. But make no mistake: These were African scholars.

And when I discovered this truth, that the faith wasn't handed to us by outsiders but was cultivated, questioned, and lived out by people whose soil we share, I was changed. Let me introduce you to some important African Christians that helped shape our faith.

Origen of Alexandria (ca. 185–254)

When I was younger, I thought theology was something for ivory towers—abstract debates about doctrines that had little to do with real life. What I learned later was that some of the deepest theological reflections were about how to know God better. The first man born on African soil that I want to introduce was Origen.

Origen of Alexandria was born around 185 in Egypt. His questions helped lay the foundation for everything that came after. What struck me wasn't just how much he wrote—it was how he wrote. He wasn't trying to win arguments. He was trying to know God.

In a moment where so many young Black believers are deconstructing what they've been taught—sorting through what's true, what's toxic, and what's been twisted—Origen's life felt strangely familiar. He didn't just accept inherited answers. He pressed in. He asked bold questions. And for him Scripture wasn't just a rulebook—it was a doorway into the mystery of life.

He taught that the Bible spoke on many levels: historical, moral, and spiritual. You could read a story and find meaning on the surface—and then read it again and find something that pierced your heart. Origen gave permission to search the text for truth that transforms, not just informs. And that opened up something for me. It helped me see that wrestling with Scripture isn't a threat to faith—it's the path of faith.

He was also one of the first to attempt what we'd now call "systematic theology." His book *On First Principles* tried to map the contours of Christian belief long before the Nicene Creed was written. Yes, some of his ideas were later challenged or corrected—but the courage it took to step into uncharted territory and try to articulate the mystery of God? That still inspires me.

And he didn't just write from a place of safety. Origen suffered for what he believed. During the Decian persecution, he was imprisoned and tortured. He never recanted. He died shortly after his release, carrying the scars of conviction in his body.

For me, Origen is a reminder that the early church's theology isn't reserved for one culture, one continent, or one type of intellect. It belongs to anyone bold enough to ask: Who is God, really? And what does it mean to follow Jesus when the answers aren't easy?

Today, when many are walking away from faith because the versions they inherited feel shallow or dishonest, Origen points to a different kind of discipleship—one that welcomes questions, honors depth, and insists that true knowledge of God must also lead to love.

Tertullian of Carthage (ca. 160–225)

Early in my theological studies, I assumed that all the important voices came from Europe. I didn't know that one of the earliest—and boldest—theologians to shape the church's doctrine came from the continent I called home. His name was Tertullian.

Born around 160 in Carthage, present-day Tunisia, Tertullian was a lawyer by training and a fighter by nature. His writing didn't tiptoe around tough issues—it confronted them head-on. And something clicked when I began reading his work. His was grounded, fierce, and unmistakably African.

Tertullian was the first Christian thinker to write extensively in Latin, which would later become the dominant language of Western theology. That alone reshaped Christian thought for centuries. But what really caught me was this: He was the one who gave us the word *trinitas*—Trinity.

The very way we talk about God today—one being, three persons: Father, Son, and Holy Spirit—was shaped by the pen of an African theologian. That floored me. I'd heard the doctrine of the Trinity preached all my life, but no one had told me the foundation was laid in North Africa.

But Tertullian is also remembered as a defender of the faith. While Roman authorities were trying to silence and crush the early church, Tertullian was writing bold public defenses. He showed that Christians weren't threats to the empire—they were citizens of a higher kingdom, calling the world toward justice, holiness, and hope.

Later in life, he joined the Montanist movement, which emphasized prophecy and moral rigor. Some disagreed with that turn. But his earlier contributions never lost their force. Later theologians like Athanasius and Augustine stood on the ground he cleared.

For me, his life offered something of a mirror. His legacy is a reminder that the Black church's passion for clarity, for truth, for holy living didn't start in storefront churches or revival tents—it was there from the beginning. Tertullian was doing apologetics before seminaries existed. He was defending the faith in the streets and courts of Carthage long before "Christian theology" was bound in European textbooks.

His story belies the idea that theology grew only in European cathedrals—it was also hammered out on African soil, by African hands, under the pressure of empire and persecution. And that's part of *your* inheritance.

Cyprian of Carthage (ca. 200–258)

Cyprian of Carthage may be the most relevant ancient voice for our time. He lived in the third century, more than 1,700 years ago. But as a bishop leading through political unrest, church division, and public crisis, Cyprian sounded less like a distant historical figure and more like a pastor who understood what it meant to lead through chaos.

Cyprian believed that the church wasn't just a loose collection of believers—it was a family. A body. A people bound together by love, covenant, and shared mission. His famous line still lingers: "He cannot have God for his Father who does not have the Church for his mother."[4] I'll be honest, that used to make me uncomfortable. In a world where many of us are wrestling with the church's failures, those words can feel like pressure. But as I learned more about his context, I realized he was writing during times of persecution, division, and confusion, and it hit me differently. Cyprian wasn't protecting power. He was pastoring through pain.

He offered the early church a way to navigate one of its hardest questions: What do we do with people who faltered under pressure? Those who renounced their faith to survive? Those who broke? Instead of closing the door, Cyprian opened it. He taught that repentance wasn't weakness—it was the way back to wholeness. And restoration wasn't compromise—it was the gospel lived out.

As a Black pastor watching people walk away—not from God, but from a church that no longer felt like home—I saw in Cyprian's writings a road map for reconciliation, a theology that made room for both truth and grace. He took holiness seriously—but he never forgot compassion.

Cyprian helped shape the way the church thinks about leaders. Bishops were not power brokers but shepherds—people charged with holding the body of Christ together when everything threatened to tear it apart. That vision reminds me that leadership isn't about preserving an institution at the expense of caring for people, especially when they're fractured, fearful, or forgotten.

Cyprian's legacy is faithful, not flashy. And his story reminds us that unity isn't cheap. It's forged in fire. Not by erasing differences, but by refusing to give up on one another.

Aurelius of Carthage (ca. 392–430)

While not as well known as Augustine or Tertullian, Aurelius of Carthage played a crucial role in shaping African Christianity during the late fourth and early fifth centuries. Serving as bishop from around 392 to 430, Aurelius was a key ally of Augustine and hosted several church councils in Carthage that helped define early Christian doctrine.

But what makes Aurelius particularly powerful for me was his courage. During a time when the Roman Empire was persecuting Christians and targeting African clergy, Aurelius defended the rights of the poor and the marginalized. He consistently stood against the Donatists—*not* to silence dissent, but to preserve the unity of the African church under persecution.

In a time when Christianity was becoming politicized, Aurelius didn't compromise. He was an African bishop serving African communities, helping establish a tradition of theological leadership and spiritual resilience that still speaks today.

Athanasius of Alexandria (ca. 296–373)

The first time I learned about Athanasius, what struck me wasn't just what he wrote—it was what he endured. Here was a man from North Africa mocked by his opponents as the Black Dwarf—an insult aimed not just at his stature but at his skin. It was an attempt to discredit his leadership and undermine his voice. But Athanasius didn't flinch.

He was the bishop of Alexandria during one of the fiercest theological battles of the early church. Arianism was spreading—a teaching that claimed Jesus was created by God and wasn't fully divine. To some, it might've sounded like theological hairsplitting. But Athanasius saw the danger clearly: If Jesus wasn't God, then the gospel unraveled. Redemption depended on Christ being both fully human and fully divine.

His response was pastoral. In his masterpiece *On the Incarnation*, he wrote about a God who became flesh to heal what humanity had broken. He wasn't writing for academics. He was writing to hold the center of the faith together.

That moved me. He wasn't some distant scholar in a tower—he was a pastor who bled for what he believed. He stood firm, even though the emperors in power sided with his enemies. He was exiled five times for defending the truth. Five times. But he kept coming back. That kind of conviction challenges me even now. Would I stand that strong?

In many church traditions, we recite this part of a creed—"True God from true God, begotten not made, of one substance with the Father." Athanasius shaped that. He fought for it. And he did it not in Rome or Constantinople but in Africa.

And that matters.

Because, growing up, I never knew that one of the most important defenders of the gospel came from a place people often treat like a theological footnote. But once I saw it, I couldn't unsee it. The African roots of Christian theology weren't a side story. They were central.

Athanasius reminds us that truth doesn't always come from the powerful or the palatable. Sometimes it comes from the margins—from people the empire tries to silence. His life teaches us that orthodoxy isn't just about words on paper. It's about holding fast to the truth of who Jesus is, even when it costs you everything.

And maybe that's why his story speaks so clearly now. Because we're still asking: Who gets to define Christianity? Who gets to shape the center? Athanasius answered with his life: The gospel isn't Western. It isn't white. It's rooted in truth, forged in struggle, and defended by people the world tried to ignore.

Didymus the Blind (ca. 313–398)

Didymus the Blind was in Alexandria too. Some say he was blind by the age of four. Though blind, Didymus became one of the most brilliant theologians of his time with his insights into the mysteries of God that put him at the heart of early Christian thought.

He led the famous catechetical school in Alexandria, one Origen had made legendary a century before. Didymus taught students how to think deeply, pray faithfully, and seek God with their whole minds. One of his students was Jerome—the man who would go on to translate the Bible into Latin.

What moved me about Didymus wasn't just the fact that he overcame the challenges of blindness. It was how he saw truth others missed. He was one of the first to clearly articulate the full divinity of the Holy Spirit. At a time when church leaders were still wrestling with what the Trinity meant, Didymus was already pointing to the Spirit's co-equality with the Father and the Son. He wasn't content with surface-level faith—he wanted to name, with precision and passion, the God who had changed his life.

Even when his work was later questioned because of his admiration for Origen—and his possible belief in universal restoration—his commitment to theological depth and spiritual clarity never wavered. His vision was rooted in Scripture, reason, and deep trust in the character of God.

Discovering Didymus cracked open another part of the lie I'd been taught—that deep Christian thought, the kind that shapes creeds and councils, came only from European minds. That's just not true. Alexandria—an African city—was home to one of the most important theological schools in history. And at its helm, at a crucial moment in the formation of Christian doctrine, was a blind African theologian who saw further than most.

Didymus reminds us that some of the clearest vision comes from those who've learned to trust God in the dark. His story pushes back against every lie that says Black Christians and African Christians are just recipients of theology rather than its originators.

He shows us what theological imagination looks like when it's shaped by love, perseverance, and faith refined by limitation. And his voice still echoes today—not just as a curiosity of history, but as a witness to the Spirit's power to speak through every kind of vessel.

Augustine of Hippo (354–430)

You've probably heard of Augustine. You might even have read his *Confessions* or heard sermons shaped by his teaching on grace and sin. But here's what I didn't hear growing up in church: Augustine was African.

Not just in name, but in body, in culture, and in soil.

He was born in Thagaste, in what is now Algeria, and served as bishop of Hippo—also in North Africa. His world was not the marble halls of Rome or the cathedrals of Europe but the heat, color, and tension of Roman Africa. And that matters. Because it means that one of the most important voices in the history of Christian theology emerged from a colonized African land.

The first time I really sat with that truth, it felt like something shifted. I learned that Augustine was a "church father." But no one told me he could have been my father—someone whose story bore traces of my own. His mother, Monica, was a praying African woman. His younger years were marked by restlessness, a search for identity, and the pull of competing influences. And when he came to faith, it wasn't just intellectual—it was transformative.

Augustine didn't just write theology—he wrestled with it. In *Confessions*, he poured out the struggle of his heart, not hiding behind academic distance but naming his failures, his longings, his questions. In *City of God*, he offered a bold vision of hope beyond the crumbling political systems of his day—reminding believers that their true citizenship was not Rome but God's eternal kingdom. Those ideas have shaped Christian faith for more than 1,500 years.

He was also right in the middle of some of the most heated theological debates of his time. Augustine had to help a fractured church answer a difficult question: What happens when a pastor sins? Does it cancel out the sacraments? His answer—that God's grace, not human perfection, makes the church holy—became a theological anchor in Christian tradition.

Reformers such as Luther and Calvin would later call Augustine one of their greatest influences. But what they rarely said out loud was that they were drawing from the mind of an African man.

For too long, Augustine's identity was recast—flattened into a Roman, a European, a generic church father. But reclaiming his Africanness is about more than geography or skin tone. It's about telling the truth. It's about restoring what was erased. And for those of us who've been told that theology isn't ours—that our job is to sit in the pews while others explain God to us—Augustine's story says otherwise.

He wasn't a footnote in someone else's tradition. He was a giant in ours.

Reclaiming Augustine isn't about pride. It's about placement. It's about remembering that our faith isn't borrowed. It's rooted. And the more we recover the voices that sound like ours, the more we can see that we belong—not on the margins of the gospel, but at its center.

Shenoute of Atripe (ca. 360–450)

Shenoute changed what I thought I knew about monks and monastic life. I had been taught to imagine monastic life as quiet and removed from the world. But Shenoute wasn't quiet. And he didn't retreat. He led one of the most powerful spiritual communities in Africa—*and* he used that position to confront injustice head-on.

Shenoute served as abbot of the White Monastery in Upper Egypt during the fourth and fifth centuries. He wrote in Coptic, not Greek or Latin, and shaped what we now know as Coptic Orthodox Christianity—not from the sidelines, but from the center. His sermons and letters were unflinching. He called out corrupt landowners who exploited the poor. He rebuked unjust leaders, defended the oppressed, and demanded that believers live with integrity. Shenoute understood that the gospel wasn't just a message for heaven—it was a call to transform how people lived together on earth.

That stopped me in my tracks. Because here was a North African church father who saw monastic life not as an escape but as resistance. In a society riddled with inequality, Shenoute built a community rooted in justice, shared labor, prayer, and accountability. He created what we might now call a gospel-driven social order—where holiness was measured not by isolation but by how deeply people cared for one another.

More than a preacher, he was a reformer. And when theological conflicts swept through the church, especially around the Council of Chalcedon, Shenoute stood firm. He defended the Alexandrian tradition of Christ's full divinity and full humanity, helping shape the distinctive Christology of the Coptic Church. He fought to preserve a theological identity grounded in both truth and tradition—unshaken by imperial politics or outside pressures.

Shenoute reminds us that Africa's contributions to Christianity were never one-dimensional. The same continent that gave us Origen's theological brilliance and Augustine's sweeping vision also gave us Shenoute's courageous voice—rooted in the people, responsive to their pain, and relentless in calling the church to holiness and justice.

For those of us wrestling with whether Christianity can still be trusted, Shenoute stands as a challenge and an invitation. The faith we inherited has always had voices like his—bold, rooted, and unafraid to call the church back to what it's meant to be.

He didn't whisper from the desert. He roared.

Frumentius (early fourth century)

Frumentius is often called the "Apostle to Ethiopia," and with good reason. His story is one of providence, resilience, and Spirit-led leadership. According to early church historian Rufinus of Aquileia, Frumentius and his brother Aedesius were young men when their ship docked on the Red Sea coast—and everything changed. They were taken captive and brought to the royal court of Aksum, in what is now Ethiopia and Eritrea. But instead of disappearing into obscurity, they rose in influence and gained the trust of the king.

After the king's death, Frumentius became an adviser to the queen regent. And even in that delicate position, he made space for faith. He supported Christian merchants, encouraged worship, and opened the door for the gospel to take root in royal circles. Sensing the moment, Frumentius traveled to Alexandria and appealed for oversight. There, Athanasius of Alexandria, the same bishop I introduced previously who defended Christ's full divinity at Nicaea, ordained him the first bishop of Aksum and sent him back to nurture this growing movement.

Under Frumentius's leadership, Christianity spread through the Aksumite empire. When King Ezana eventually declared it the state religion in the mid-fourth century, Ethiopia became one of the first Christian nations in the world. What Frumentius helped plant would grow into the

Ethiopian Orthodox Tewahedo Church, a community of faith with more than 1,600 years of unbroken history, worship, and witness.

His story confronts the colonial myth head-on. Christianity didn't come to Africa on slave ships or at the end of a European spear. Long before colonizers claimed to bring the gospel, Africans were already receiving it, interpreting it, and embedding it in the life of their people. Frumentius didn't arrive as a conqueror. He arrived as a servant—and his legacy is still alive in one of the oldest Christian traditions on earth.

Frumentius reminds us that the spread of the gospel in Africa wasn't dependent on political power or institutional might. It grew through relationship, humility, and a God who works through the unexpected. And that's good news for anyone who's ever felt like an outsider or wondered whether their place in the story mattered.

Pachomius and the Birth of Monastic Community

I assumed, like most people, that Christian monasticism was a European invention. To be honest, I hadn't thought much about it. But names such as Benedict of Nursia came up in church history textbooks, and the image of monks praying in stone abbeys somewhere in medieval Europe stuck with me. Then I came across a name I'd never heard before: *Pachomius*. And that changed everything.

Pachomius was an Egyptian Christian, born around 292, who had once served as a Roman soldier. What caught my attention wasn't just that he founded one of the earliest monastic communities—it was *why* he did it. At a time when some believers were withdrawing from society to pursue solitude in the desert, Pachomius imagined holiness could be forged in community, not isolation. And not just any community, but one centered on justice, humility, discipline, and mutual care.

His first monastery, established around 320 in Tabennisi on the banks of the Nile, became a spiritual ecosystem. It wasn't an escape from the world—it was a reordering of it. There were rhythms of prayer, work, silence, Scripture, and shared meals. Everyone contributed. Everyone served. They didn't live apart from suffering—they responded to it by building a space where no one was above another. This was an alternative social order grounded in the gospel.

And here's where the connection hit me: After spending so much time studying how Christianity was used to prop up hierarchy, justify slavery, and reinforce systems of dominance, discovering Pachomius felt like stumbling onto a blueprint for something better. In a world where the church had so often bowed to power, Pachomius built a community where the powerful had to kneel. Where no one hoarded wealth. Where leaders were chosen by character, not class. Where dignity was shared, not earned. It was, in its own way, a form of resistance—a quiet but radical rejection of empire values in favor of kingdom ones.

Discovering this, I had to pause. Why had no one told me that a Black man from Africa had pioneered a model for Christian communal life? The roots of monasticism went deep beyond the European cathedrals and into the deserts of Upper Egypt. The "rule of life" that shaped Christian spirituality for centuries—Eastern and Western—began with Pachomius.

He influenced Basil of Caesarea, one of the great Eastern theologians, who adopted Pachomian ideas when crafting his own monastic rules. Later, Benedict of Nursia would write his famous *Rule of Saint Benedict*, which echoed Pachomius's principles of shared labor, hospitality, and worship. But those who imitated his structure often left his name and continent behind.

Pachomius wasn't an academic. He built communities where theology took on flesh—in the way people ate, prayed, worked, and lived together. His monasteries became places of refuge, dignity, and renewal. In a world marked by Roman hierarchy and violence, he modeled something different: the kingdom of God, practiced daily.

And that legacy isn't lost. To this day, the Coptic Orthodox Church in Egypt maintains vibrant monastic communities in the very deserts Pachomius once walked. His story reminds me that Africa didn't just *receive* the Christian faith—it organized it. Structured it. Lived it. Passed it on.

For me, learning about Pachomius was more than a history lesson—it was a reclaiming. It taught me that our faith has always had African hands shaping it. And it made me wonder: What else have we forgotten?

Ethiopia: One of Christianity's First Homes

For too long in my understanding, Christianity's roots ran only through Rome, Geneva, or London. But Ethiopia tells another story. A story that doesn't just add to Christian history but challenges how that history has been told.

Ethiopia's Christian identity runs deeper than most people realize. Before much of Europe had even heard the name of Jesus, believers in the kingdom of Aksum were already worshiping, baptizing, and building a distinctly African expression of the faith.

In the fourth century, King Ezana officially embraced Christianity, making Ethiopia one of the first Christian nations in the world. His faith was shaped by Frumentius, the bishop commissioned by Athanasius of Alexandria, whom we met earlier. But what's often missed is this: Ethiopia didn't passively receive the gospel. It wove the message into its cultural identity, shaping a national faith that would endure for more than a thousand years.

Out of this emerged the Ethiopian Orthodox Tewahedo Church, a tradition rich with prayer, music, fasting, and liturgy. Its services are still conducted in Geʿez, a sacred language preserved for worship across generations. The church's calendar, hymns, theology, and iconography reflect not just theological rigor but the creativity and resilience of African devotion.

And then there's Lalibela.

High in the Ethiopian highlands, the rock-hewn churches of Lalibela defy imagination. Carved directly from volcanic stone in the twelfth and thirteenth centuries, these eleven churches form a pilgrimage site unlike any in the world. They weren't constructed by importing materials or laying bricks—they were revealed by removing everything that wasn't holy. According to tradition, King Lalibela envisioned them as a "New Jerusalem" for those unable to reach the Holy Land. And they're still active today. Pilgrims walk barefoot through sacred halls. Prayers are still chanted in Ge'ez. The gospel is alive in stone.

But Ethiopia's witness goes beyond architecture. When Islam spread across North Africa in the seventh century, many Christian centers faded or adapted. Ethiopia stood firm. Its autonomy protected its libraries, its monasteries, its theology. Through invasions, droughts, and isolation, Ethiopian Christians kept the faith. Their survival wasn't accidental—it was intentional. And their story reminds us that faithfulness doesn't need foreign validation to be real.

This isn't just an interesting fact—it's a theological correction. Ethiopia's story reminds us that Christianity didn't begin in Europe, and it never belonged exclusively to the West. The gospel has always had African fingerprints—inked in manuscripts, etched in stone, sung in ancient tongues, and passed down through communities who never let go of the hope they received.

And Ethiopia is only one thread in a larger African tapestry.

Across the continent, the early church flourished in many languages—Greek, Latin, Coptic, Ge'ez—and took on many forms. Some communities practiced radical desert monasticism. Others opened theological schools in bustling cities. Still others passed down truth through liturgy and oral tradition. This wasn't a single story. It was a symphony.

That diversity is a strength. It reminds us that the body

of Christ was never meant to be colorless or uniform. It was meant to be multilingual, multiethnic, and deeply rooted in every soil it touched—including African soil.

And once you know this, you can't unsee it. Ethiopia doesn't just preserve history. It reframes it. It challenges every assumption that says the faith had to be handed to us by someone else. It shows that we were never just recipients—we were cultivators. Carriers. Builders. Believers.

This is the inheritance we weren't taught—but it's ours to reclaim.

I'm not Ethiopian Orthodox myself—and I know most of us reading this come from Protestant, Baptist, or non-denominational traditions. So this isn't a call to change denominations. But I do believe their legacy holds something we need. The Ethiopian church reminds us that Christianity was flourishing in Africa long before it reached Europe or America. It offers a living counternarrative to the lie that Christianity is a white man's religion. We don't have to become Orthodox to be inspired by their witness. Their presence is a reminder that our faith has deep African roots—and that reclaiming our story doesn't mean abandoning the gospel. It means recognizing that we were there all along.

Why a Faith Rooted in African Soil Matters to Me

For many of us, the image of Christianity as the "white man's religion" still lingers. It's what some of our elders heard growing up. It's what some of our peers are saying now. And after centuries of colonization, slavery, and silence from too many pulpits, it's not hard to understand why. The faith that was meant to free became, for many, a tool of control. That wound runs deep.

But that's not the whole story.

Africa was there at the beginning—not as an afterthought, but as a foundation. The gospel didn't just arrive on the continent with slave ships and colonial flags. It took root in African soil long before that. And when I began learning this—not just in theory, but in detail, name by name, story by story—it did something to me. It helped me hold the weight of the harm and the hope at the same time. It gave me language for a faith that felt both honest and holy.

Because once you see that the first person baptized after Pentecost was an African government official . . . once you realize that Christian theology was shaped in Alexandria, Carthage, and Hippo . . . once you find out that the word *Trinity* was first coined in Latin by a North African thinker . . . you can't unsee it. You start to feel it in your bones: This isn't a borrowed faith. It's an inherited one.

But that phrase—"coined in Latin"—can be misleading. Too often, the use of Latin has caused African voices to be mistaken for European ones. Thinkers such as Tertullian, Cyprian, Augustine, and Aurelius lived and ministered in North Africa, yet their theological writings were absorbed into the tradition of Western Christianity and stripped of their African context. Why? Because they wrote in Latin—the official language of the Roman Empire. In cities such as Carthage and Hippo, elite education, public life, and church governance were conducted in Latin, even though the people themselves were of Berber, Punic, or other African ancestry.

These leaders were shaped by African soil, African questions, and African communities—but Rome's language became the medium of their message.

And that's where the erasure began. Over time, as European scholars curated the story of the church, they centered Rome and sidelined Africa. They imagined the early church as a European story told in Latin rather than a global movement that included vibrant African voices from the very beginning. Figures such as Aurelius and Augustine were painted in European tones—literally and figuratively—until their African heritage faded from the page. And the African origins of their theology were all but forgotten.

But language doesn't erase lineage. Latin may have shaped the grammar of their thought, but it didn't define their identity. These weren't outsiders to the faith—they were architects of it. When we recover their full story, we see the truth: The so-called Latin church was deeply African. And reclaiming that truth helps us dismantle the lie that Christianity is white by origin or inheritance.

Knowing that changes how I read Scripture. It changes how I understand my place in church history. It changes how I pastor. It changes how I parent.

When I stand before my congregation, I don't just teach them about Augustine, I tell them: He was African, like you. When someone tells me Christianity is the white man's religion, I don't argue—I tell them about the rock-hewn churches of Lalibela and the monks of the Egyptian desert and the theological schools of Alexandria. I tell them about the long line of Black believers who didn't just survive history—they shaped it.

And I think of you.

Maybe you've felt like a visitor in church spaces that were supposed to be home. Maybe you've heard your Blackness treated as something to overcome instead of something God delighted to create. Maybe your questions were met with shame. Maybe your history was never mentioned. Maybe you were told—explicitly or subtly—that Christianity was something you had to adopt, not something you already belonged to.

But I want to say to you what I had to learn to say to myself: You were always part of this story.

The gospel didn't start in Europe. The church didn't grow up in white seminaries. The cross wasn't first carried by conquerors. In fact, it was first carried by Jesus, and then by a Black man named Simon, a man from Cyrene—a city in North Africa. And your presence in the church isn't a diversity initiative—it's a homecoming.

That matters because the version of Christianity we've inherited in the West often leaves us with a fractured sense of belonging. It tells us we can have Jesus but not our story. We can have salvation but not our skin. We can belong to the church—but only if we leave our questions at the door.

But reclaiming our history allows us to reject that lie.

When we remember the faith of our African ancestors—not just their suffering, but their wisdom, their worship, their theology—we begin to see Christianity as it truly is: global, multiethnic, rooted in justice and liberation, not just in personal piety. We stop asking whether we belong, and we start living like we do.

This isn't about nostalgia. It's about restoration. It's about recovering what colonization tried to erase and what silence tried to bury. And it's about offering our children a better story—one that doesn't ask them to choose between Christ and their culture but shows them how the two have always been intertwined.

I still believe the gospel is good news. And Africa's witness is one of the reasons why it's not just good news. It's not a white man's religion!

So if you're still holding the question "Can this faith be mine?" let me offer you the answer I found in the archives, in the Scriptures, and in my own bones: It already is.

FIVE

Faith-Fueled Resistance

IN THE PREVIOUS CHAPTER, I TOOK US back to the roots of our faith in African soil. We uncovered a Christianity that was alive and growing long before it ever reached European shores. But now I want to fast-forward. Here I will show you how that same faith took root in the resistance of enslaved people, sharecroppers, freedom fighters, and everyday believers who dared to trust that God was on their side. These weren't just quiet churchgoers—they were theologians in motion. They shaped a faith that could hold grief and grit at the same time. A faith that didn't just survive oppression—it defied it. And, in doing so, they reminded the world that the gospel isn't the property of the powerful. It's a lifeline for the oppressed.

I've learned important truths about my faith from the

quiet resolve of those who refused to give up. I've seen elders who carried both a Bible and a protest sign. I've heard it in the voices of freedom songs that rise from pain but are stitched with defiant hope. I've felt it in the tension of preaching a gospel that both saves and unsettles—one that speaks of heaven, yes, but also demands justice on earth.

The more I sit with our history, the more I recognize that Black faith has carried a double burden—not because it was foreign to us, but because it was distorted around us. This faith was present on African soil long before slavery, yet in America we encountered a version weaponized to justify our dehumanization. Still, we didn't abandon Jesus. We clung to the truth underneath the lies. We reclaimed what was already ours, even when others tried to chain it.

From Christianity's beginning, the faith has lived in tension—used at times to justify domination, and at other times to defy it. Black Christian witness carried that tension over the centuries.

A painful irony in our story is that the same faith that was twisted to defend slavery also gave birth to movements of resistance, dignity, and hope. In the hands of the oppressed, the Bible became a lifeline. They found in its pages the voice of a God who sees, who hears, and who delivers.

From Nat Turner's rebellion to the Civil Rights Movement, Black Christians have turned to Jesus not as the champion of the status quo but as the liberator of the poor. The gospel was more than a message of personal salvation—it became a call to action, a summons to break chains and challenge injustice in God's name.

Here, in these acts of sacred defiance, we glimpse the redemptive power of the faith—not as oppressors handed it down, but as it was reclaimed by those who knew in their bones that God stands with the oppressed.

"Let My People Go": The Faith of Nat Turner

Nat Turner's story is one of faith forged in the crucible of oppression. Born into slavery in Southampton County, Virginia, in 1800, Turner was recognized early on for his intellect and spiritual sensitivity. His enslaver's son owned a complete Bible and, in a rare act, allowed Turner to read it. That access changed everything.

As Turner studied Scripture for himself, he didn't encounter a gospel of submission. He met the God of Exodus—the one who thundered through Moses, "Let my people go" (Ex. 5:1). He found psalms that cried for deliverance, prophets who stood toe-to-toe with kings, and a Messiah who came to "proclaim freedom for the prisoners" (Luke 4:18). For Turner, this wasn't poetry—it was prophecy. As he later described it, "I heard a loud noise in the heavens, and the Spirit instantly appeared to me and said the Serpent was loosened, and Christ had laid down the yoke he had borne for the sins of men."[1]

His enslavers thought the Bible would make him compliant. But once he read it in full, it made him dangerous. Turner came to see his faith not as a tool for survival but as a call to deliverance. "I was intended for some great purpose," he told Thomas R. Gray, the lawyer who transcribed his confession.[2]

On August 21, 1831, Turner led what became known as the Southampton Insurrection. Over the course of two days, he and his followers moved from plantation to plantation freeing enslaved people and taking direct action against those who upheld the system of slavery. Turner believed the rebellion was a divine mandate. He saw signs and visions in the heavens and felt that God had confirmed his role as a prophet and deliverer. "I communicated the great work laid out for me to do, to four in whom I had the greatest confidence," he explained, framing the insurrection as a spiritual mission.[3]

Though the rebellion was brutally suppressed and Turner was eventually captured and executed, his legacy endured. For abolitionists, he became a symbol of both the horrors of slavery and the deep theological conviction it inspired in resistance. Historian Vincent Harding explains that Turner's faith was inseparable from his fight for freedom; he envisioned the very farms and fields of Virginia as the place where God's kingdom would break the power of the slaveholders, and he saw himself as a chosen instrument in that struggle.[4]

Nat Turner's life is a testament to the liberating power of Scripture in the hands of the oppressed. He reminds us that, even in bondage, Black Christians read the Bible not through the lens of domination but with the eyes of the exodus. Faith did not mean passivity—it meant prophetic action.

And that's where it gets personal for me.

When I first read Turner's story in depth—not just

about the rebellion but about the Scriptures that fueled it—I remember feeling a kind of holy discomfort. It wasn't just his courage that struck me. It was the way he read the Bible. Not as a tool for personal blessing, but as a call to collective deliverance. I'd grown up with a strong sense of faith, but Turner helped me understand that Black faith has always held a double burden: We were handed a gospel that others hoped would tame us, and we turned it into a force they couldn't contain.

Turner's story challenges me as a preacher, as a man, and as a Black Christian. It reminds me that our faith isn't just about enduring pain. It's about confronting it. It's about refusing to let the silence of slaveholders or the fear of consequences strip the gospel of its power to liberate.

This is our legacy. Sacred defiance. Holy resistance. A faith that both saves souls and breaks chains.

Harriet Tubman: A Legacy of Resistance and Liberation

Harriet Tubman is one of American history's most enduring symbols of courage, resistance, and moral clarity. Born into slavery around 1822 in Dorchester County, Maryland, she escaped bondage and went on to lead hundreds of others to freedom as a conductor on the Underground Railroad. Tubman's legacy is not only that of a freedom fighter but also that of a beacon of hope, justice, and determination in the face of systemic oppression.

But in recent years I've noticed something troubling—her story, like those of so many other Black heroes, is being slowly erased from some textbooks, softened in school curricula, or reduced to a single line in a unit on slavery. The irony is painful. In a nation that owes so much to her moral clarity, we're watching a quiet campaign to sideline the very truth she risked her life to proclaim.

Tubman's fight for liberation began with her own escape from slavery in 1849. Despite the personal risks, she returned to the South at least thirteen times to lead approximately seventy enslaved people to freedom. Her courage and cunning earned her the nickname "Moses," likening her to the biblical figure who led the Israelites out of bondage. Tubman used a sophisticated network of safe houses, covert routes, and trusted allies to navigate the Underground Railroad, one of the most dangerous systems in American history.

But her resistance didn't stop there. During the Civil War, Tubman served as a nurse, scout, and spy for the Union army. In 1863 she became the first woman in US history to lead an armed military operation—the Combahee River raid—which resulted in the liberation of more than seven hundred enslaved people. After the war, she continued her advocacy, championing women's suffrage and working tirelessly to support formerly enslaved individuals. Her life is a testament to strategic brilliance, moral fortitude, and an unshakable belief that God is on the side of the oppressed.

Tubman's life shaped me before I ever read her full

biography. I grew up hearing about her in passing—always with reverence, always with awe. But it wasn't until I was older that I really sat with her story. The more I read, the more I understood how active her faith was. She didn't just believe in God—she trusted him enough to walk back into danger, again and again, to free others.

She wasn't a pastor. She didn't preach sermons. But she lived theology with a clarity that many pulpits never reach. She believed God would lead her even when the path was dark. And she believed her people were worth saving, not someday in heaven, but right now on this earth. That kind of faith still convicts me.

Today, Tubman's story is increasingly at risk. Some political movements push to restrict the teaching of slavery and systemic racism in schools, claiming that these topics are "divisive." In that climate, Harriet Tubman becomes dangerous again—not because she's armed, but because she tells the truth. Her life refuses to let us forget what this nation was built on—and what it takes to build something better.

To erase or diminish Harriet Tubman's place in history is to lose sight of what justice and freedom mean. Her story is not just about overcoming hardship; it is about resistance, organization, and unwavering dedication to dismantling systems of oppression. Preserving her legacy isn't just about honoring her—it's about honoring all of those who resisted in ways big and small, those whose names we'll never know.

Tubman reminds us that faith is not passive. It's not a

private comfort. It's a public witness. Her story calls us to courage, to action, and to truth telling—even when the cost is high. And it's a reminder to every Black Christian who has ever felt the weight of this country's contradictions: You come from a line of people who didn't wait for freedom to be handed to them. They fought for it, prayed through it, and made a way when there was no way.

That's our legacy. And it's one worth fighting to remember.

The Abolitionist Witness

As the abolition movement gained momentum, Christian theology became one of its most powerful tools. Abolitionists turned to Scripture, not to justify the status quo, but to confront it. They dismantled pro-slavery arguments by reclaiming the Bible as a sacred text of justice, not oppression.

Figures such as Harriet Beecher Stowe and William Lloyd Garrison wielded Scripture as a weapon against the moral rot of slavery. Galatians 3:28—"There is neither Jew nor Gentile, neither slave nor free"—became a rallying cry for human dignity. Stowe's *Uncle Tom's Cabin* was more than a novel; it awakened the nation's conscience, revealing bondage's spiritual and ethical cost. Abraham Lincoln is said to have greeted her as "the little lady who made this great war"—a testament to the cultural impact of her work and the theology woven through it.

While much of this resistance came from Black

Christians and churches, it's important to acknowledge that white Christians also played vital roles—risking their reputations, livelihoods, and, in some cases, their lives to stand against slavery. Though they were not the majority, their solidarity helped shape a moral coalition rooted in the gospel's call to justice.

I remember the first time I stood in a sanctuary where an abolitionist meeting had taken place. The pews were worn with age, the windows plain but dignified. And I found myself wondering—what did it feel like to preach freedom in a nation that still called slavery a divine institution? What kind of courage did it take to believe that the gospel not only saved souls but also shattered chains? It struck me then that the same Bible used to enforce obedience had been weaponized for freedom by those bold enough to read it through the eyes of the oppressed.

Abolitionist faith wasn't limited to words. It drove action—bold, costly, embodied resistance. Beyond individual acts of defiance, churches became engines of protest. Abolitionist societies met in sanctuaries. Sermons denounced slavery as sin. Congregations organized rallies, distributed antislavery literature, and lobbied for legal change. For these communities, the fight against slavery wasn't just political—it was spiritual. It was a test of faith and a call to action.

Faith gave the abolition movement its moral firepower. It provided clarity in the face of contradiction and resilience in the face of fear. It reminded those in the struggle that their cry for freedom echoed the voice of God.

The Civil Rights Movement

When the Church Walked: The Montgomery Bus Boycott

The Civil Rights Movement didn't appear overnight. It grew out of the spiritual foundation laid by abolitionists and freedom fighters who had long turned to faith as a source of strength and direction. For many in Montgomery, Alabama, faith wasn't just personal but public. It didn't sit quietly in pews. It marched, boycotted, and bore witness.

That witness took center stage on December 1, 1955, when Rosa Parks refused to surrender her bus seat to a white fellow passenger. Parks wasn't acting on impulse. As a devout Christian, active NAACP member, and longtime advocate for justice, she saw her quiet refusal as an act of moral conviction. "I would like to be remembered as a person who wanted to be free," she later reflected, "so other people would be also free."[5] Her arrest mobilized the Black community, igniting a 382-day bus boycott that would become a model of nonviolent resistance.

Churches were at the heart of it all. Sanctuaries became strategy rooms. Pulpits became platforms for protest. Pastors preached hope and justice, even when threats loomed. Week after week, gatherings reminded people that they were not alone—that their struggle mattered, and that God was with them. What might have been a passing protest became a movement rooted in conviction, community, and a gospel big enough to confront Jim Crow.

Preaching Justice, Living Peace: Dr. King's Leadership

Dr. Martin Luther King Jr. didn't just speak against injustice—he preached through it. A Baptist minister formed in the Black church tradition, King saw his calling as both spiritual and political. He read the prophets—Amos, Isaiah, and Jeremiah—and believed their cries for justice still thundered through the streets of Montgomery and Birmingham. "Let justice roll down like waters," he quoted from Amos 5:24, "and righteousness like a mighty stream."[6]

His sermons and speeches, like the "Letter from Birmingham Jail," argued for civil rights and declared a gospel. He refused to separate love from justice. King wrote to white clergy who had urged patience: "Injustice anywhere is a threat to justice everywhere."[7]

As president of the Southern Christian Leadership Conference, he embraced nonviolence—not as weakness, but as moral courage. He found inspiration in Gandhi, yes, but filtered that wisdom through the life and teachings of Christ. "Christ furnished the spirit and motivation," he explained, "while Gandhi furnished the method."[8]

At the heart of his vision was the "beloved community"—a world where love would overcome hate and justice would roll down like waters. King didn't just imagine that world. He invited others to build it—not only with protest signs and policy demands, but also with prayer-soaked courage and a faith that refused to stay quiet in the face of oppression.

The Black Church Was the Engine

Throughout the Civil Rights Movement, Black churches were command centers for justice, sanctuaries for the weary, and classrooms for courage. These congregations became the movement's heart and soul, offering far more than Sunday sermons. They offered strategy, strength, and spiritual sustenance.

When the streets became dangerous and hope ran thin, churches opened their doors for mass meetings and late-night organizing sessions. In the basements of Baptist sanctuaries and the fellowship halls of AME congregations, everyday people mapped boycotts, printed flyers, and planned marches—often knowing full well the risks they faced. These were sacred spaces where freedom was not just preached but practiced.

Worship services were more than rituals; they were rehearsals for resilience. Hymns such as "We Shall Overcome" became anthems of endurance, sung with a defiance that echoed through the walls and into the streets. Preachers stood in the pulpit and reminded their people that justice was not just a political goal but a divine calling. Sermons lit fires that no water hose could extinguish.

Out of these pews and pulpits of churches rose leaders. Men and women who had sharpened their voices in choir stands and their convictions in prayer meetings became the architects of a movement. In the Black church, Dr. King learned to speak with both fire and grace, Fannie Lou Hamer found her holy boldness, and so many unnamed organizers were nurtured and sent.

The church was not on the sidelines of the movement—it was its engine. And its legacy reminds us what happens when faith becomes fuel for freedom.

Reading this history as a pastor, I feel a deep tension in my chest because this inheritance came at a cost.

These stories are inspiring and convicting. The courage of Rosa Parks, the prophetic voice of Dr. King, the grit of Black churches that stood firm when everything around them shook is our spiritual lineage. And yet we also carry the weight of what they endured. The bomb threats. The cross burnings. The silence of those who claimed the same Jesus but couldn't see our pain.

Can we hold both—the beauty and the burden? The strength of our ancestors' faith and the scars it had to carry?

We must.

Because to reclaim our faith we have to tell the whole story. Not just of our suffering, but of our sacred resistance. Not just of the harm done in Jesus' name, but of the hope kept alive in his name. The Civil Rights Movement shows us that the gospel can still speak, still lead, still liberate—when we are bold enough to live it out loud.

Let's keep going.

Theologians Who Carried the Flame

Not all resistance was carried out on the streets. Some of it was forged in sermons, essays, and late-night seminary classrooms—where the questions ran deep and the wounds were still fresh. While the Civil Rights Movement surged forward, a parallel theological movement began to take shape.

Its goal wasn't just to support the struggle—it was to name its sacred roots. To remind us that liberation was not a political trend but a gospel calling.

Howard Thurman gave the movement its contemplative soul. In *Jesus and the Disinherited*, he wrote not for the powerful but for what he called "those with their backs against the wall. . . . They are the poor, the disinherited, the dispossessed."[9] He reframed Jesus as a poor, oppressed Jew living under empire—a Savior who knew firsthand what it meant to be marginalized. Thurman's writings helped leaders such as Dr. King embrace nonviolence not just as strategy but as spiritual discipline.

James Cone, often called the father of Black liberation theology, picked up that mantle and wrote with righteous fire. In *Black Theology and Black Power*, he gives insight to his readers that there would be no Black liberation theology without black oppression and dehumanization. It was birthed in the black power movement, emphasizing Black identity, dignity, worth, and freedom. The term *black power* was first used in the civil rights movement in the spring of 1966 by Stokely Carmichael to designate the only appropriate response to white racism.[10] Cone was clear: A faith that refused to stand with the suffering was not true to Christ. His theology was bold, unsettling, and rooted in the lived experience of Black people who had endured centuries of religious hypocrisy. Some of his later writings would stir debate, especially in how he engaged whiteness. But to understand Cone, you must understand the pain he was responding to—the betrayal by those who claimed to follow Jesus but upheld systems that crucified Black dignity.

Benjamin Mays, longtime president of Morehouse College, offered a different kind of theological resistance—one shaped by scholarship, mentorship, and moral courage. He often reminded his students, "It is not enough to be good; you must be good for something."[11] This phrase became a hallmark of his teaching and was a recurring exhortation in his speeches at Morehouse. Mays preached a faith that moved. His sermons shaped minds and lit hearts on fire. His mentorship of Dr. King and others planted seeds that would blossom in courtrooms, churches, and city streets.

Reading these voices reminded me: Our resistance wasn't a political movement that borrowed the language of faith. It was a faith movement from the start—one that dared to believe the gospel had something to say about housing and prisons, about education and dignity, about power and the cross.

These theologians were freedom fighters. And even when we wrestle with some of their conclusions, we can still honor the courage it took to speak out when silence was safer.

Lives That Preached Without a Pulpit

What Thurman, Cone, and Mays put into words, others lived out in action. Their theology took flesh in blistered feet, bruised bodies, and bloodstained Sunday clothes. For many, faith was what got you through the march, the jail cell, the courtroom, the beatdown. Here are three who showed us what it means when faith walks into the fire.

Fannie Lou Hamer: Singing in the Storm

I'll never forget the first time I heard Fannie Lou Hamer's voice—raw, ringing, and holy. She didn't sound like a politician or preacher. She sounded like someone who knew suffering firsthand and still believed God was listening. Beaten in a Mississippi jail for trying to register to vote, Hamer didn't lose her song. She sang spirituals through swollen lips and cracked ribs. "His eye is on the sparrow," she said, "and I know he watches me."

Hamer's faith gave her fire. When she testified at the 1964 Democratic National Convention, she wasn't just recounting injustice—she was prophesying. Her words pierced through the polished rhetoric of politicians and laid bare the brutal reality of Black life in America. She often said, "I'm sick and tired of being sick and tired." But even that exhaustion was soaked in a hope that ran deep. She believed a just God could still make crooked paths straight—and she gave her life to that work.

Ella Baker: Power to the People

Ella Baker didn't want a microphone—she wanted a movement. She believed that God gave gifts to the whole community, not just the charismatic few. And that belief shaped everything she did. Raised in the AME Church, Baker understood discipleship as empowerment. She mentored young leaders and helped birth the Student Nonviolent Coordinating Committee, one of the most effective grassroots organizations of the movement.

She didn't speak from a pulpit, but her theology was

unmistakable: Strong people don't need strong leaders. That's a gospel statement if I've ever heard one. She believed the Spirit moved in ordinary folks—in sharecroppers, students, and struggling mothers. And she lived her faith by making sure the spotlight never stayed on her.

John Lewis: Good Trouble, Holy Ground

John Lewis was the youngest speaker at the March on Washington, but his wisdom came from an old well. Trained in nonviolence as a sacred discipline, Lewis saw getting into "good trouble" as an act of discipleship. When he crossed the Edmund Pettus Bridge in Selma and faced state troopers, he wasn't just making a political point. He was walking into danger because his faith told him love is stronger than fear.

I've listened to his words from that day, and each time I'm struck by the quiet resolve in his voice. "We do not want our freedom gradually, but we want to be free now!" he declared.[12] That's not bravado—that's belief. Belief that suffering is not the end of the story. Belief that justice is not just a political ideal but a spiritual mandate. His skull was cracked by a club, but his hope never wavered.

Faith That Still Speaks

When I look at the lives of Fannie Lou Hamer, Ella Baker, and John Lewis, I don't see just history—I see a kind of faith that refuses to flinch. A faith that doesn't retreat when the cost gets high. These unperfect people were faithful ones. They believed—deep in their bones—that God was on the side of the oppressed, and they lived like it. Their stories remind me that our faith has never been fragile. It's been forged in fire. And if you've ever wondered whether Christianity is worth holding on to, remember this: The same gospel that was once weaponized to shackle us has also been the song that sustained us. That's not blind tradition. That's sacred resistance. And it's still ours.

Legislative Victories: When Faith Becomes Law

The Civil Rights Movement wasn't just about changing hearts—it was about changing laws. For generations, Black faith communities prayed, marched, and protested with the hope that their struggle would shape a more just society. And eventually the walls began to crack.

Each legislative victory was more than policy—it was the public harvest of private pain and sacred perseverance. Behind every law was a lineage of worship and witness.

I think of those midnight church meetings where elders strategized by candlelight. I think of deacons who guarded the sanctuary doors during mass meetings. I think of the young folks who walked to school through threats and spit because their families believed change was possible. And I can't help but wonder—what prayers did they whisper as they walked? What scriptures did they carry in their spirit?

The Civil Rights Act of 1964 ended legal segregation and made it illegal to discriminate in public accommodations and workplaces. When President Johnson signed the bill, Dr. King stood behind him—but make no mistake, the law was written in the streets long before it reached the Senate floor. The act was the result of years of grassroots organizing, marches, and direct action that pushed Congress to respond to the demands of the movement.

The Voting Rights Act of 1965 tore down the barriers that had kept our people from the ballot box for generations. That law wasn't birthed in Washington—it was birthed on a bridge in Selma, in blood and prayer. When John Lewis was beaten on Bloody Sunday, he wasn't carrying a weapon. He was carrying a gospel that said, "Let justice roll down like waters."

The Fair Housing Act of 1968, passed days after Dr. King's assassination, tried to address the racism baked into our neighborhoods. It came too late for many—but it came. And it bore the fingerprints of those who believed that God cares not just about where we worship but also about where we live.

Each of these laws—and the many that followed—stand as echoes of faith made flesh. They remind us that the gospel is not just a personal message. It's a public one. It refuses to stay in the sanctuary when the streets are burning. It calls us not only to believe but to build.

And that's what our ancestors did. They built. With worn shoes and holy rage. With spirituals and strategy. With a Bible in one hand and a protest sign in the other.

As Ella Baker once said, "The major job was getting people to understand that they had something within their power that they could use."[13] That power—rooted in God—moved a nation.

So if you've ever questioned whether your faith still matters in a world so broken, look at what it already made possible. You carry the legacy of people who turned belief into policy. Who turned suffering into structure. Who turned hope into law.

This wasn't the work of politicians alone. It was the work of a praying people, a preaching people, a persevering people. And their story is your inheritance.

Let no one tell you your faith is weak. It helped remake the law of the land.

Still Marching: Faith and Today's Justice Movements

The spirit of faith-fueled resistance continues to stir in today's justice movements, drawing strength from the deep wells dug by abolitionists, freedom fighters, and civil rights leaders who came before us. Their legacy was etched into the soul of the church. They left us more than memories. They left us a model.

A model of protest that prayed. A model of theology that marched. A model of love that did not shrink from confrontation.

Though many wrestle with aspects of his theology, voices like James Cone's carried that legacy forward, declaring that God does not stand above suffering—he stands with the oppressed. "The scandal is that the gospel means liberation, that the God of Israel is a God of the oppressed and the downtrodden."[14] Cone's theology didn't just speak to pain—it named it, challenged it, and rooted resistance in the liberating power of Jesus.

We hear echoes of that theology today. The phrase "Black lives matter" emerged not just as a political statement but as a spiritual cry—a lament, a plea, a declaration in a world too often deaf to Black dignity. And as Christians we affirm this truth without hesitation: Black lives do matter. Not because culture says so, but because God does. Every person bears the *imago Dei*—the image of God—and that image demands honor.

At the same time, we approach every movement with discernment. While we affirm the heart cry for justice embedded in the phrase "Black lives matter," we recognize that not every organizational platform aligns with the gospel. Our ultimate allegiance is not to any movement or political agenda but to Christ. And our commitment is to a justice shaped by biblical theology, love, truth, humility, and the sacred worth of every human life.

A Faith That Still Sets Us Free

From Nat Turner's fire to Harriet Tubman's courage, from Montgomery's bus stops to the steps of the Lincoln Memorial, faith walked with our people. It was a faith not of submission but of uprising. It was not a gospel of escape but one of liberation.

And that same gospel calls to us still.

It calls us to continue the struggle with boldness. To see Christianity not through the lens of comfort or control but through the cross. To reclaim a faith that doesn't bow to power but dares to speak hope in the face of injustice.

So if you've ever wondered whether this faith could be yours—whether it still has the power to heal what history broke—hear this: It does.

It always did.

And it still sets people free.

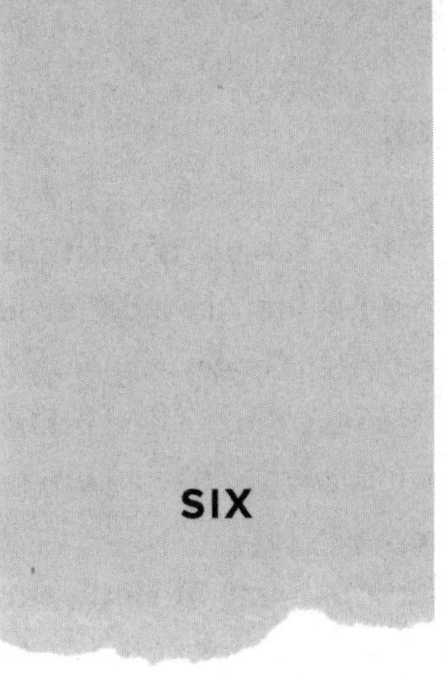

SIX

The God Behind the Resistance

WE'VE SEEN HOW BLACK CHRISTIANS across generations resisted injustice, not just with protest signs or political demands, but with Scripture in their hands and fire in their bones. The prophets of our tradition—Fannie Lou Hamer, Benjamin Mays, Howard Thurman, James Cone—drew from biblical conviction. Their fight was rooted in the character of the God they served. Because once you see who God really is, justice becomes the only faithful response.

That's what this chapter is about.

If the people we've just met were shaped by the Bible—if

they risked their lives because of what they believed God required—then we need to take a deeper look at that God. Not the God of sanitized Sunday school stories. Not the God used to bless oppression. But the God behind the resistance. The God whose justice runs like a current through every page of Scripture.

Justice is not a footnote in God's story. It's the beat that undergirds his every move—the rhythm of his reign, the ground beneath his throne. From the very beginning, God's justice wasn't an afterthought—it was the plan. The through line. The fire in the bones of prophets, the melody in the psalms, the heart of the law, and the warning in every judgment.

So when we talk about justice, we're not talking about a political trend or a social media moment. We're talking about who God is. At his core.

Scripture doesn't give us a vague ideal. It gives us a God who acts. "The Lord is a God of justice," Isaiah writes plainly (Isa. 30:18). Moses calls him "a faithful God . . . upright and just" (Deut. 32:4). And the psalmist lays it bare: "Righteousness and justice are the foundation of your throne; love and faithfulness go before you" (Ps. 89:14). If you want to draw near to God, you can't avoid justice. It's part of the path.

And this justice? It's not cold. It's not detached. It shows up in how God defends the widow, welcomes the stranger, and hears the cry of the oppressed. It's rooted in compassion and expressed through action. Justice in Scripture always has a face. A name. A story.

But I know what you might be wondering—because I've asked it too:

- If God is so committed to justice, then why does it feel so rare?
- Why do the guilty go free while the innocent bear the weight?
- Why does the system protect power and ignore pain?
- Why do we keep praying to a just God while watching injustice run loose?

The answer doesn't lie in God's absence. It lies in our apathy.

Justice hasn't disappeared. We've just stopped looking for it in the places it's supposed to live—in our churches, our relationships, our policies, our daily discipleship. Too many who claim God's name have let justice become optional. Decorative. Political. Disposable.

But here's the truth: If justice is central to who God is, it has to become central to who we are.

So let's not settle for talk.

Let's meet justice again—at the feet of the one who never stopped doing it.

Justice Is Who God Is

If you've made it this far, you've already seen the pattern. Black Christians didn't invent justice as a side cause to our faith—we turned to it because it was already written in the heart of God.

The civil rights leaders, freedom fighters, and spiritual voices we just read about didn't stand for justice in spite of their faith. They stood because of it. Because their Bibles were open. Because their God was just.

That's the thread I want to pull now.

If you didn't get this the last time I wrote it, when we talk about justice, we're not talking about a political trend or a social media moment. We're talking about who God is.

Moses didn't call God "the Rock" just because he is strong. He said it because God is unwavering in his righteousness: "The Rock, his work is perfect, for all his ways are justice. A God of faithfulness and without iniquity, just and upright is he" (Deut. 32:4 ESV).

The psalmist backed it up: "Righteousness and justice are the foundation of your throne; love and faithfulness go before you" (Ps. 89:14).

These aren't throwaway lines. They're the clearest picture we get of God's character.

The Hebrew word *mishpat*—translated as "justice"—shows up more than two hundred times in the Old Testament. And it's not just about legal rulings. *Mishpat* is about lifting up the oppressed, holding the powerful accountable, and making sure no one gets pushed to the margins—especially not the widow, the orphan, the immigrant, or the poor.

That's not some ancient ideal. That's your grandmother praying for rent money. That's your cousin pulled over for no reason. That's your people navigating a world built to keep them out.

Old Testament scholar Bruce Waltke puts it like this:

"The righteous are willing to disadvantage themselves to advantage the community; the wicked are willing to disadvantage the community to advantage themselves."[1]

That hits different when you've watched people hoard advantage while telling you to wait, be patient, or forgive and move on.

In the New Testament, the Greek word *dikaiosyne* wraps justice and righteousness into one. Jesus uses it in the Beatitudes: "Blessed are those who hunger and thirst for righteousness [*dikaiosyne*], for they will be filled" (Matt. 5:6). Paul carries the thread, showing how being made right with God means living right with others (Rom. 1:17; 3:21–26).

And as Dr. Eric Mason reminds us, "More than half the books of the Old Testament mention justice directly. You can't read the prophets, the Psalms, or even the laws of Moses without hearing God's concern for equity and fairness ring loud and clear."[2]

God's justice is not just punishment—it's protection. It's restoration. It's repair.

Listen to the Scriptures cry out with you:

- "Do not deny justice to your poor people in their lawsuits" (Ex. 23:6).
- "Follow justice and justice alone, so that you may live" (Deut. 16:20).
- "Do not pervert justice; do not show partiality to the poor or favoritism to the great, but judge your neighbor fairly" (Lev. 19:15).

- "David reigned over all Israel, doing what was just and right for all his people" (2 Sam. 8:15).
- "The Lord loves righteousness and justice; the earth is full of his unfailing love" (Ps. 33:5).
- "Learn to do right; seek justice. Defend the oppressed. Take up the cause of the fatherless; plead the case of the widow" (Isa. 1:17).
- "This is what the Lord says: 'Maintain justice and do what is right'" (Isa. 56:1).

This isn't just a call to punish what's wrong. It's a call to restore what's right.

As philosopher and theologian Nicholas Wolterstorff puts it, "Justice is the enjoyment of one's due. And what is due is the enjoyment of shalom, of flourishing in all dimensions of existence."[3]

You've been told to pray, forgive, move on. But God says justice matters. He says your hunger for equity and repair is justified. You're not imagining things. You're echoing the very heart of God.

So if you've ever wondered where God stands when the scales are off—know this: He stands with you.

Justice at the Heart of Jesus' Mission

If you ever doubted whether justice belongs at the center of our faith, just look at Jesus. From the very beginning of his public ministry, he made his priorities clear. He didn't start with a parable. He didn't launch a healing crusade. He walked into the synagogue in his hometown, unrolled the scroll of Isaiah, and declared:

> The Spirit of the Lord is on me,
> because he has anointed me
> to proclaim good news to the poor.
> He has sent me to proclaim freedom for the prisoners
> and recovery of sight for the blind,
> to set the oppressed free.
>
> —LUKE 4:18

That wasn't a metaphor. That was his mission statement.

Jesus didn't treat justice like an optional add-on to spiritual life. It *was* the life. He preached good news that lifted the poor. He healed bodies and welcomed outsiders. He set people free—spiritually, yes, but also socially, economically, and emotionally. The same Jesus who forgave sin also flipped tables in the temple. He called out injustice with clarity and compassion. He didn't just comfort the broken—he confronted the systems that broke them.

You don't have to stretch Scripture to see it. It's right there, woven into the gospel.

In Matthew 23, Jesus rebukes the religious leaders—not for abandoning the law, but for using religion to dodge justice. They tithed their spices with precision, but "neglected the more important matters of the law—justice, mercy and faithfulness" (Matt. 23:23). Let that land. You can be scrupulously religious and still miss God—if you ignore justice.

Then, in Matthew 25, he speaks of the final judgment—and where does he place himself? Not with the powerful, but with "the least of these." The hungry. The stranger. The prisoner. And he says plainly: Whatever you did or didn't do for them, you did or didn't do for *me* (v. 40).

That's not just a call to charity. That's a revelation: Christ identifies with the oppressed. He binds himself to the wounded and the weary. He doesn't just *care* about justice—he *embodies* it.

Eddie Byun puts it this way in his book *Justice Awakening*: "Are they hungry? Feed them. Are they naked? Clothe them. Are they oppressed? Set them free. Are they fearful? Protect them."[4] That's not a campaign. That's discipleship.

Justice in Jesus' ministry wasn't theoretical. It showed up in his touch, his timing, his tables. He healed the woman no one would touch. He sat with the tax collector no one would eat with. He waited for the Samaritan woman no one would talk to. And he never once asked them to erase who they were in order to be seen, healed, or loved.

He saw their whole story. Named their pain. And still invited them into new life.

That's the Jesus we follow.

Justice and the Image of God

If justice is central to God's character, then it must also shape how we see one another. Because at the root of justice is this truth: Every human being carries the *imago Dei*—the image of God.

That's why justice isn't just about systems. It's about sight.

It's about seeing your neighbor, not as a threat, not as a problem to be fixed or a project to be pitied, but as sacred. Worthy. Bearing divine imprint.

Jesus didn't come just to adjust laws. He came to restore sight—to help us see rightly. To see God in the ones we've been taught to overlook. To recognize the holy in the faces of the hungry, the hurting, and the historically excluded.

And that changes everything.

Because once you realize that every person you meet carries the image of the God who does justice, then injustice becomes more than a political issue. It becomes a spiritual crisis. A distortion of God's design. An offense not just against people but against the God who made them.

So as we move forward, keep this in mind: The fight for justice is never just about fairness. It's about reverence. It's about reclaiming the sacred dignity that God wove into your Black skin—and into every person created by his hand.

That's where we go next.

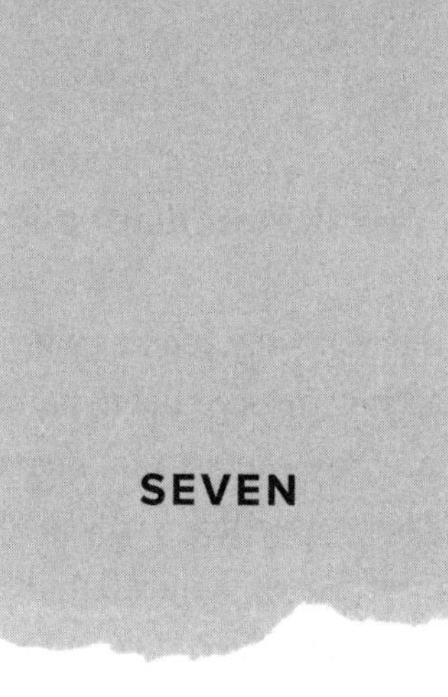

SEVEN

Every Person Is Made in the Image of God

IT WAS A FRIDAY NIGHT. MY COUSIN HAD just dropped off his son, still in his scrubs from his hospital shift. The kids were playing outside, and we were planning a movie night. I told them I'd run to the store to grab some snacks. I threw on my all-black Kobe Mamba sweatsuit and hopped into my wife's brand-new car—still with dealer plates and the registration visible in the window.

Not even five minutes later, I saw the same police cruiser that had driven by and waved at my kids moments earlier. This time, they made a U-turn and lit up their sirens. At first, I thought they were headed somewhere else, so I pulled over to let them pass. But they didn't pass. They pulled up behind me. Fast.

Before I could even fully process what was happening, one officer kicked his car door open, hand on his weapon, slapping the side of my car, yelling, demanding I roll my windows down. The other officer flanked the passenger side, where my cousin sat frozen, hands flat on the dashboard. I kept mine on the steering wheel. I wasn't about to give them any excuse.

I calmly explained that I wasn't reaching for anything. I told them the registration was in the window. The officer wasn't hearing it—until his partner, who had a little more sense, finally said, "It's fine. I can see him." That moment should've de-escalated the situation. It didn't.

It was only when I asked, "You don't remember me, do you?" that something shifted. My cousin jumped in: "You just waved at our kids outside. That's our house." The officer's face changed. He realized who I was. I said, "You had a meeting at our church last week. I'm the pastor."

Now, let me ask you: Why did it take all that?

Why did he have to see my church, my degrees, my connections before he saw my humanity?

The truth is, when he looked at me, he didn't see a pastor. He didn't see a father. He didn't see a professor. All he saw was my Black skin—and, in his eyes, that was enough to presume I was a threat.

That's the wound.

That's the lie this chapter has to confront.

Before the world ever labeled me dangerous or disposable,

God looked at me and called me *good*. Before I was a pastor, before I had titles, before I earned degrees, I bore the image of God. So did my cousin. So do you.

And when that truth is ignored or erased, it's not just a matter of bad theology—it's a matter of life and death.

There are truths so sacred, so foundational that everything else must be built on them. One of those truths sits quietly at the beginning of the Bible, yet it echoes through every struggle for dignity and freedom: Every person is made in the image of God.

That's more than a theological idea. That's good news. It means God's love didn't wait for you to clean up or measure up. It was there from the very beginning. That divine fingerprint on your soul is what racism tries to erase—and what God refuses to let be forgotten.

For many of us, this truth wasn't first encountered in a theology book—it was lived. It was the reason our grandparents endured segregation with heads held high. It was what allowed enslaved people to believe they were more than property. It's what gives today's freedom fighters the courage to say we matter—not because society says so, but because God does.

The doctrine of *imago Dei*—being made in the image of God—is not just religious language. It is the soil from which justice grows. It tells us that our value isn't earned by achievement or erased by oppression. It was breathed into us by the Creator himself.

To affirm that truth is to take a stand against systems that degrade. Against narratives that dehumanize. Against any theology that makes peace with inequality. In this chapter I want to talk about that sacred image and what it demands of us.

The *Imago Dei* in Today's English

Right there in the first chapter of Genesis—before sin enters the world, before any laws are given, before there are nations or skin tones or social hierarchies—we get a breathtaking declaration: "Let us make mankind in our image, in our likeness" (Gen. 1:26).

That one sentence changes everything.

It means you were never an afterthought. You weren't created for someone else's use or to play a lesser role in someone else's story. From the very beginning, you were made to reflect something of God's own nature.

You, brothers and sisters—you were stamped with his image.

That truth is more than religious poetry. It's the foundation of your worth. You don't have to earn dignity. The world doesn't get to assign your value—or take it away. It was placed on you by God himself.

When I first began to really grasp this—not just read it, but let it hit me—I remember sitting with the weight of it. The *imago Dei* means that my Blackness isn't an accident. It means my life isn't something to be tolerated or explained away. It means my presence on this earth reflects the creativity and intention of the Creator.

And it doesn't stop with me.

This isn't just about self-worth—it's a calling. If every person carries the image of God, then every person deserves to be treated as sacred. That includes the neighbor who's hurting. The protester who's been silenced. The stranger whose name we've never learned. The child who's overlooked. The man society tries to break down.

To affirm the *imago Dei* is to commit to seeing people the way God sees them—and acting like it.

It's not just a doctrine to believe. It's a mission to live.

When you speak up for someone who's been dehumanized, you're honoring the image of God in them. When you challenge systems that strip people of their dignity, you're living into your original design. When you look in the mirror and refuse to let anyone tell you you're less than—because you know who made you—you're walking in holy defiance.

Not abstract theology. Not Latin terms. But a truth that's as real as your breath.

You were made in the image of God. So was your brother. So was your sister.

And that changes how we see the world—and how we move in it.

Universal Human Dignity

The image of God in every person means that human dignity is inherent. It is not earned through performance or granted by society. Each life carries sacred value from the moment of creation, not because of what we do, but because of who created us.

That's not just a comforting truth—it's a disruptive one.

The *imago Dei* challenges us to see one another as God sees us, without the distortion of bias or the ranking of human worth. Where society builds ladders and labels, God's image levels the ground. This truth cuts through the hierarchies that place some lives above others, insisting that dignity is not something to be earned but something bestowed—freely and irrevocably—by God.

Systematic theologian Millard Erickson affirms, "Because all are in the image of God, nothing should be done which would encroach upon another legitimate exercise of dominion. . . . Everyone has a right to exercise dominion—a right, which ends only at the point of encroaching upon another's right to exercise dominion."[1] In other words, anything that manipulates, coerces, or oppresses another image-bearer is not only unjust—it is theologically indefensible.

This sacredness of life runs through the story of Scripture. Genesis tells us that all humanity shares a common origin. We are not strangers or adversaries—we are kin. We are tied together by the divine imprint we each bear. That shared lineage is not just a biological fact—it is a theological foundation for equality, calling us to resist anything that seeks to divide or diminish.

Paul echoes this in Galatians 3:28: "There is neither Jew nor Gentile, neither slave nor free, nor is there male and female, for you are all one in Christ Jesus." In a world obsessed with categories, status, and supremacy, this declaration still cuts like a sword. It dismantles systems of exclusion and calls us into a deeper unity—one grounded not in sameness but in shared sacredness.

But the fact that we bear God's image is more than a truth to affirm. It is a responsibility to live. As image-bearers, we must reflect God's character—his love, mercy, compassion, and justice. These are his *communicable attributes*—the divine qualities he shares with us and calls us to embody.[2] To bear God's image is to carry his heart into the world—to stand with the vulnerable, lift up the marginalized, and ensure everyone is treated with the dignity they've carried since creation.

At the same time, we recognize what is not ours to carry—his *incommunicable attributes*. God alone is omnipotent, omniscient, and omnipresent.[3] That distinction keeps us grounded. It reminds us that while we're called to reflect God's character, the work of ultimate justice, restoration, and healing is sustained by his power, not ours.

We're compelled to act when we grasp what it means to bear the *imago Dei*—not just with personal morality but with public responsibility. We become not only recipients of dignity but guardians of it, on behalf of others. That means resisting systems that strip people of their worth. It means advocating for laws, communities, and institutions that reflect the justice and mercy of our Creator. Because honoring God's image in others is not optional for those who bear it themselves.

Impact on Racial Justice

The doctrine of *imago Dei* stands as a direct rebuke to racial injustice. For centuries, systems of oppression have depended on a single lie—that some people matter more than others. Slavery, segregation, and systemic racism were built on the brutal denial of human worth, reducing God's image-bearers to property, labor, or threat. That lie has echoed across generations, not just in laws and policies, but in hearts, habits, and institutions.

The Constitutional Compromise and the Three-Fifths Clause

Perhaps no example more starkly illustrates this dehumanization than the infamous three-fifths compromise embedded in Article I, Section 2 of the United States Constitution. This provision declared that enslaved Black persons would be counted as "three fifths of all other Persons"[4] for purposes of taxation and representation in Congress. As constitutional scholar Akhil Reed Amar notes, "The three-fifths clause was a clear expression of the framers' willingness to sacrifice human equality on the altar of political expediency."[5]

The clause was not, as some mistakenly suggest, a statement that Black people were only three-fifths human; rather, it was a political compromise between Northern and Southern states over how to count enslaved persons for congressional representation and direct taxation. The Southern states, seeking to enhance their political power, wanted slaves counted fully for representation while denying them any political rights. Northern delegates resisted counting people who had no rights at all. The resulting compromise reduced the South's political power compared to counting enslaved people fully, while still providing the Southern states with significant additional representation based on people they systematically oppressed.

Frederick Douglass, the abolitionist and former slave, recognized the profound theological contradiction in this arrangement, declaring in 1852: "What, to the American slave, is your 4th of July? I answer: a day that reveals to him, more than all other days in the year, the gross injustice and cruelty to which he is the constant victim. . . . There is not a nation on the earth guilty of practices, more shocking and bloody, than are the people of these United States, at this very hour."[6]

While the clause was not technically a statement about the inherent worth of Black people, this constitutional provision nonetheless codified their systematic exclusion from full political personhood into America's founding document, creating a political system that gave additional power to slave states based on the very people they enslaved. The compromise remained in effect until the Fourteenth Amendment effectively nullified it following the Civil War. The three-fifths clause thus embodied a fundamental contradiction in the founding of America—a nation proclaiming liberty and equality while explicitly reducing the political personhood of enslaved people to enhance the power of their oppressors.

The *Imago Dei* as Resistance

The *imago Dei* refuses to bend to those lies. It declares—without qualification—that every person carries the image of God. That every life is sacred. That no one is disposable. Howard Thurman, the influential Black theologian, has articulated this divine truth powerfully: "The contradictions of life must be faced honestly and courageously. They are not resolved by the pious repetition of magic words. In the most concrete and practical sense, God is Spirit seeking incarnation in the human."[7]

This truth unmasks the foundations of racial hierarchy. It refuses to let skin color, language, or heritage define human value. Scripture does not permit the elevation of one group over another; it insists that we are all equally stamped with divine worth. That includes those whom the world has pushed to the margins, silenced, or vilified.

Black leaders throughout American history have consistently invoked this theological principle to counter constitutional betrayals. Sojourner Truth's famous question—"Ain't I a woman?"—was fundamentally a claim to full humanity in the face of intersectional oppression. Martin Luther King Jr. framed the civil rights struggle as a fight to realize the *imago Dei* in public life: "The end is reconciliation; the end is redemption; the end is the creation of the beloved community. It is this type of spirit and this type of love that can transform opposers into friends."[8]

The Black church has long embraced this truth as a source of strength and a standard of protest. It has preached dignity in the face of dehumanization, demanded justice where others offered silence, and proclaimed God's image in Black bodies when society tried to deny it. The doctrine of *imago Dei* was not just a theological concept—it was a lifeline, a weapon against despair, and a summons to resist.

Bishop Daniel Alexander Payne of the AME Church wrote in 1839: "We are created in the image of God. Neither color nor condition can destroy this, his image. . . . No people can be utterly degraded when they honor, love, and obey his commandments."[9] This affirmation directly countered the constitutional reduction of Black humanity and provided theological grounding for resistance.

The Continuing Work of Justice

For the church to be faithful today, it must reclaim that same clarity. It must resist every form of cultural supremacy and every structure that treats one group as less than fully human. To affirm the *imago Dei* is to challenge injustice wherever it hides—whether in housing policies, education systems, policing practices, or pews.

This work of justice is also the work of discipleship. Because when we honor the image of God in others, we honor the God who made them. As James Cone asserted: "The Gospel of God's revelation in Jesus Christ is not identified with white culture. The Gospel is God's message of liberation for the oppressed of the land, the affirmation that Jesus has made our history, our struggle, God's own."[10]

From the three-fifths compromise to contemporary manifestations of racism, the contradiction between America's professed ideals and its treatment of Black

Americans remains a theological challenge. The doctrine of *imago Dei* continues to call us to a higher standard—one that recognizes divine worth where human systems have denied it.

Bearing God's Image in the World

The *imago Dei* must be affirmed and embodied. In a world fractured by injustice, rivalry, and fear, this sacred truth calls us to something deeper: to see the face of God in one another, to honor the divine imprint etched into every life, and to live in ways that reflect his mercy, justice, and love.

The more we grasp this truth, neutrality is no longer an option. We cannot remain passive in the face of dehumanization. We will be compelled to speak when others are silenced, to rise when others are pushed down, to confront the systems and habits that rob image-bearers of dignity.

Because this is the church's calling: not to protect comfort, but to proclaim worth; not to preserve ease, but to embody Christ. Not to retreat into silence, but to bear witness. The world does not need a church that merely recites the doctrine of *imago Dei*—it needs a church that lives it with courage, tenderness, and truth.

Let that be our witness. A people who know they bear God's image—and live like it matters.

PART 3

Becoming the New Body

WE'VE NAMED THE PAIN. WE'VE WRESTLED with the truth.

Now comes the question that won't leave us alone: So what now?

If we stopped here, we'd be left with a mirror—full of honesty, but offering no direction. But this book was never just about looking back. It's about reclaiming the future. And for us that future starts with something Jesus prayed for with his whole heart: that we would be one.

Not the kind of oneness that erases difference. Not a fragile peace that demands your silence. But a holy unity—born through honesty, repentance, and the radical work of love.

This final part is where we walk that road together.

You're going to hear hope—not cheap optimism, but the

kind of hope that rolls up its sleeves. The kind that rebuilds what injustice tried to destroy.

Because we're not just trying to fix the past. We're called to build something new.

Part 3 is about living as the beloved community. Not just an idea—but a people. A people shaped by grace, committed to repair, and determined to reflect the heart of a Savior who tore down every dividing wall.

So take a breath. This is the path forward—not easy, but sacred. Not perfect, but possible.

Let's walk it together.

EIGHT

Oneness

I REMEMBER THE HOPE IN HIS VOICE WHEN he told me what they were planning. Bishop Kenneth Ulmer, my "Pops," was trying to build something rare. A bridge.

He and a white pastor from Orange County had agreed to bring their churches together in the name of unity and reconciliation. One predominantly Black church from Inglewood. One predominantly white church from Orange County. The idea was bold, even beautiful. And, for a moment, it looked like the kingdom.

Pops gathered hundreds of our members—Black families from the city—and they made the drive. Nearly an hour on the freeway to show up for reconciliation. Nearly every seat in that sanctuary in Orange County had a person in it. Black and white faces, and other races, worshiping side by side. Pops said it started to look like heaven.

But then came the return visit.

The plan was for the white pastor to bring his congregation to Inglewood. But before the Sunday even arrived, the phone rang.

"I don't know how to tell you this," the pastor said, "but . . . my people will not drive down there. They won't drive to Inglewood! They just won't do it!"

That was it. No theological explanation. No plan to try again. Just . . . they won't come.

At that moment, all I could hear was the old line about Jesus—"Can anything good come from Nazareth?"

Only this time it was "Can anything good come from Inglewood?"

And the answer, it seemed, was no.

That day, the truth hit hard: For some, reconciliation was fine as long as it didn't require sacrifice. As long as it didn't disrupt their comfort. As long as it didn't mean going where they didn't want to go.

I used to think reconciliation was the end goal. But in my experience it has too often been reduced to an event. A photo op. A shared worship night. A handshake across the aisle.

But oneness? Oneness is not an event. It's a lifestyle.

A lifestyle of unity with siblings in Christ from different backgrounds and ethnicities. A way of living that stretches beyond Sunday services and into real relationships. One that mirrors the heart of God and embodies his dream for his people—not just gathered, but truly united.

What Oneness Really Means

And I'll be honest with you: I didn't always believe oneness was possible. Not after seeing the way our churches remain divided. Not after sitting through "racial unity" events that ended in silence or sidesteps. Not after living in a faith tradition that often made me feel as though I had to choose between being Black and being Christian.

But then I started paying attention to what Scripture actually says. Not the superficial unity we talk about in statements and slogans, but the Spirit-formed, blood-bought oneness that Jesus died to make real. A kind of community that doesn't just tolerate difference but is made whole by it. A people drawn together not by politics or background or comfort but by Christ.

Ephesians 2 stopped me in my tracks. Paul helped me see a vision for unity that went beyond polite coexistence. He revealed the kind of unity that tears down walls—literal and spiritual. The kind that makes family out of former enemies. The kind that says to both the privileged and the excluded: "There's room for you here—but not as you were. Something new has to be born."

So now I have to ask you what I had to ask myself: If we've reclaimed our faith, if we've confronted its distortions and recovered our roots—what do we do next?

This chapter is my answer.

There Were Walls in the Bible Too

Paul doesn't ease into this truth—he goes straight for it. Writing to gentile believers in Ephesus, he tells them to *remember.* Not to guilt them, but to ground them in what grace has done: "Therefore, remember that formerly you who are Gentiles by birth and called 'uncircumcised' by those who call themselves 'the circumcision'" (Eph. 2:11).

That word *uncircumcised* wasn't just a label. It was a wound. In first-century Jewish culture, circumcision marked you as a covenant insider. It meant you belonged to the promises that God gave to Abraham, that you were part of a people with a sacred calling. To be called *uncircumcised* was to be reminded you didn't belong. It was a slur that carried theological weight and cultural sting.

Jewish-gentile division ran deep. The language of "insider" and "outsider" wasn't just in people's hearts—it structured entire communities. *Uncircumcised* became shorthand for impurity, inferiority, and exclusion. The walls between people were real and religion often reinforced them.

Then Paul, with pastoral precision, lays it bare in verse 12. This is what being on the outside looks like:

- Separated from Christ
- Excluded from citizenship in Israel
- Foreigners to the covenants of promise
- Without hope
- Without God in the world

That's not just spiritual isolation—it's social exile. These believers were barred from temple worship, denied access to Israel's sacred festivals, and treated as spiritual trespassers. Clinton Arnold confirms this wasn't metaphorical: "Gentiles were not allowed access to the inner courts or the temple. A four and a half foot barrier surrounding the inner court served as a dividing wall. The Jewish historian Josephus informs us that thirteen stone slabs written in Greek and Latin stood at intervals on the barrier, warning Gentiles not to enter. Archeologist have discovered two of these tablets. The inscription reads: 'No foreigner is to enter within the forecourt and the balustrade around the sanctuary. Whoever is caught will have himself to blame for his subsequent death.'"[1]

That "dividing wall of hostility" Paul speaks of in verse 14? It wasn't symbolic. It was literal. It kept gentiles out. It reminded them daily: You don't belong in here. And behind that wall stood not just bricks but centuries of hostility—religious, ethnic, and cultural.

But Paul wasn't just naming the wall. He was announcing its demolition.

That's the shock of the gospel in this letter: The wall isn't patched, negotiated, or painted over. In Christ, it's torn down.

Jesus Tears Down Walls

Paul shifts the conversation from memory to miracle. After naming the distance gentiles once lived with, he now declares a dramatic reversal: "But now in Christ Jesus you who once were far away have been brought near by the blood of Christ. For he himself is our peace, who has made the two groups one and has destroyed the barrier, the dividing wall of hostility" (Eph. 2:13–14).

That wall—built over centuries of exclusion, superiority, and separation—didn't just fall over. Christ tore it down. It wasn't just physical architecture that came crashing down; it was the deep spiritual and social chasm between Jew and gentile. A wall built by hands and hardened by hate was dismantled by the hands that were nailed to the cross.

This wasn't just peacemaking. This was peace made flesh. As Paul says, "He himself is our peace." Not a theory. Not a temporary truce. Jesus *is* peace—not only between God and humanity, but between peoples once defined by hostility.

The cross did what no system, law, or summit ever could. It rewrote the story. Through his death, Jesus reconciled us vertically to God and horizontally to one another. The cross is the place where both reconciliation with God and reconciliation between human beings are made possible. It is not just forgiveness of sins but the creation of a new people.

This new people doesn't erase difference—it redefines belonging. The blood of Christ becomes the gateway, and his body becomes the meeting place. Paul says it plainly in Galatians 3:28: "There is neither Jew nor Gentile . . . for you are all one in Christ Jesus." Not because we've become the same, but because Christ is now our center. In him, the walls don't just crack—they crumble. And God is building something new from the rubble.

From the outside looking in, this new kind of church won't look uniform—it will look united. Different colors, cultures, and customs, all caring for one another—not in spite of their differences, but through them.

Jesus Started a New Thing

Some of us have been around church so long that certain phrases have lost their impact. They fail to get our attention when reading or listening. This passage from Ephesians 2 may be as poignant today as it was two thousand years ago. Paul's declaration in verse 15 needs our attention afresh: "His purpose was to create in himself one new humanity out of the two, thus making peace" (Eph. 2:15).

That phrase *new humanity* isn't just a fresh start—it's a radical re-creation. Paul isn't describing a patched-up version of the old divisions. He's pointing to something deeper: a new kind of human community, birthed in Christ. It echoes back to Genesis, when God formed humanity from dust and called it good. But this time it's not just creation—it's re-creation. Where history builds walls, God tears them down and builds something better. A people defined not by ethnicity, status, or gender but by the unifying presence of Jesus.

Access to the Father is no longer through the temple priesthood or based on being a Jew. Gentiles and Jews alike now gain direct access to God through the work of Christ and by the indwelling Spirit, the very presence of God with his people.[2]

What Jesus did wasn't patchwork—it was a whole new creation. He didn't just calm hostilities; he killed them. He didn't build a bridge between enemies and hope for the best. He took the two and made one. Clinton Arnold puts it this way: "Jews and Gentiles have been brought together into this one unified body where there is peace. The result of Christ's work is that he has established peace. This teaching has implications that extend far beyond Jews and Gentiles. For all who are in Christ, there are no fences, walls, or barriers that should prevent a unity that surpasses any form of cultural or ethnic distinctiveness.[3]

Jesus Doing Oneness

All through history, folks have drawn lines—sometimes in ink, sometimes in blood—to decide who belongs and who doesn't. Ethnicity. Race. Nationality. These lines have carved deep wounds into our world, and they didn't vanish with time. They're still showing up today in institutions, in attitudes, and in the spaces we inhabit.

But then Jesus steps into the scene.

In a world shaped by "us versus them," the ministry of Jesus offers something else entirely—a disruptive, healing vision that refuses to play by the rules of exclusion. One of the clearest pictures of that vision comes in John 4. It's more than just a story about a thirsty man and a woman at a well. It's a deliberate, boundary-breaking moment of oneness that we can learn from. Jesus, a Jewish man—chooses to speak, in public, to a Samaritan woman. In doing so, he dismantles generations of prejudice and ethnic barriers with a single conversation.

This wasn't a casual detour. It was a holy confrontation with everything that divides us. And it still speaks powerfully to the kind of unity Christ calls us to embody today.

To grasp the weight of John 4, you have to know the history. Jews and Samaritans had centuries of mistrust and division. The rift went back to 722 BC, when the Assyrians conquered the northern kingdom of Israel. The intermarriage that followed gave rise to the Samaritan people, and, for many Jews, that was unforgivable—a betrayal of both covenant and culture. The Samaritans had their own Scriptures, called the Samaritan Pentateuch, their own place of worship on Mount Gerizim, and their own way of life. By Jesus' time, the divide was so deep that Jews routinely took longer routes just to avoid Samaritan territory.

So when John 4:4 says, "He had to go through Samaria," it wasn't about geography. It was about purpose. Jesus wasn't lost—he was on mission.

At Jacob's well, Jesus doesn't just pass through. He stops. He sits. And he speaks—to a Samaritan woman, no less. That one moment broke three major taboos: a Jew speaking to a Samaritan, a man speaking to a woman in public, and a respected teacher engaging someone who drew water alone in the heat of the day. Her isolation likely spoke to a deeper shame, a deeper rejection. And yet Jesus meets her there—with dignity, not disdain.

And here's what matters most for our understanding of oneness: Jesus didn't ignore her past. He names it. He tells her, "You have had five husbands, and the man you now have is not your husband" (v. 18). He names the truth of her story—not to shame her, but to offer her something better. Grace doesn't skip over reality. It transforms it.

Jesus doesn't minimize her sin, but neither does he weaponize it. He holds the tension—truth and love in the same breath. In doing so, he shows us something vital about the gospel: Her race, her gender, and her broken history do not disqualify her from the love, grace, and belonging of the kingdom of God. Even as a Samaritan woman with a complicated past, she is fully seen, fully known, and still fully invited.

He offers her "living water" (v. 10). He doesn't dodge her theological questions. He doesn't ignore her pain. He honors her with conversation. He reveals his identity, not in a temple, not among his disciples, but to her. And she becomes the first cross-cultural evangelist in the New Testament.

She came with a water jar and left with a calling.

That was a real encounter of oneness. It restored identity. It reordered worship. It released purpose. And it shows us something critical about the oneness Jesus came to bring: It's personal, boundary breaking, and embodied.

When Jesus redefines worship in John 4—"True worshipers will worship the Father in the Spirit and in truth" (v. 23)—he breaks the chains of geography, ethnicity, and exclusion. He reveals a kingdom that welcomes difference and centers sincerity.

This wasn't a side story. It was a preview of the mission in full: "Go and make disciples of all nations" (Matt. 28:19).

That woman's story becomes a spark. Her testimony turns her village upside down. And her encounter with Jesus gives us a living image of the kind of oneness he died to create—a unity that stretches across every human division.

But here's what makes this even more beautiful for us today: Unity in Christ doesn't mean erasing who we are. The gospel doesn't flatten difference—it reorders it. In Christ, our primary identity is no longer bound to race, tribe, nationality, or social status. Those markers don't disappear, but they no longer divide us either. They no longer determine our place at the table. We belong because we are in him.

And this new people? It's not theoretical. It's not just something we preach—it's something we live.

Back to Ephesians with Paul

Paul's words paint a picture of what the church is meant to be: a Spirit-formed community that reflects God's original design—a people who are different, yet deeply connected, revealing the reconciling love of God to a divided world.

Paul's vision of that reconciliation is twofold:

- Reconciliation to God: No one gets in on merit. Jew and gentile alike stand in need of grace. "For through him we both have access to the Father by one Spirit" (Eph. 2:18). No back entrance. No outer court. No "wait your turn." In Christ, every one of us has equal access to the Father.
- Reconciliation to one another: That old hostility? It's not just buried—it's been put to death. "He himself is our peace, who has made the two groups one and has

destroyed the barrier, the dividing wall of hostility" (Eph. 2:14).

Miroslav Volf puts it plainly: "Justification by grace through faith excludes any and every claim to privilege on the basis of race, class, or gender. . . . All boast is excluded except the boast in the Lord."[4]

In Christ, the wall is not just broken—it's gone. The blood of Jesus doesn't just cleanse; it creates. A new people. A new way of being human. A peace not built on denial but born from the cross.

The Church as a Community of Reconciliation

In the final verses of Ephesians 2, Paul uses three powerful images to describe the new identity of those who belong to Christ—and together they reveal what the church is meant to be then and now:

- The church is made up of citizens: "You are no longer foreigners and strangers, but fellow citizens with God's people" (v. 19). No longer on the outside looking in. No longer barred by birth or background. In Christ, we are full participants in the kingdom—legal heirs to the promises once thought reserved for others.
- The church is a family: "Members of his household" (v. 19). Not guests. Not temporary boarders. Family. Brought into God's own house, named and known, with all the rights of belonging.

- The church is a temple: "Built together to become a dwelling in which God lives by his Spirit" (v. 22). That's the most intimate picture of all. Not a structure of stone or a sanctuary reserved for a few—but a living, breathing people joined together by the Spirit of God. That's the kind of church that Jesus died to create.

Each of these metaphors intensifies the reality of what reconciliation means—oneness. It's not just about diversity—it's about divine design. The church is not called to be a community where different people simply coexist. We are called to be a new kind of family: interdependent, Spirit-formed, and rooted in a love that binds us deeper than blood or background.

This isn't superficial unity or symbolic inclusion. It's the Spirit of God binding people together who once stood on opposite sides of the wall—and building something altogether new.

Living This Out, in You and Through You

What Paul lays down in Ephesians 2 is a blueprint for something new. And it starts with us. The church was meant to show the world what reconciling power looks like. But too often it didn't. It preached unity while preserving division. Recall my encounter with the Slave Bible. The church read the verses about oneness but kept on building walls.

You and I are part of the people Jesus died to make new. And our lives and communities can still reflect that vision.

Here's what it can look like, starting right where you are.

Reject Racial Superiority

You've seen what happens when spiritual privilege turns into pride—when people weaponize religion to elevate themselves and exclude others. That's not the gospel. And you don't have to carry the weight of proving yourself to anyone. As John Stott wrote, "We must not be content with paper unity. We must live it out by welcoming and honoring every believer equally in Christ."[5] That includes you.

Pursue the New Community

The "new humanity" in Christ isn't some colorblind blur. It's a mosaic—multiethnic and God ordained. That doesn't mean every church has to look like a diversity photo on a brochure. Some communities are all Black, some are all white, some are immigrant led, some are mixed—and that's okay.

But wherever you are, this truth holds: You don't have to check your culture at the door to belong to Jesus. You don't have to assimilate to be accepted. Your voice, your leadership, your gifts—they're essential to what the church is meant to be.

Living this out doesn't always mean merging churches. Sometimes it means building friendships across lines of difference. Partnering in mission. Listening and learning from one another. As Brenda Salter McNeil puts it, "Reconciliation is not an optional add-on to the gospel; it is at the very heart of God's plan to restore creation."[6]

So whether you're in an all-Black church, a multicultural ministry, or somewhere in between—you can still reflect the new humanity Christ died to create. Not by striving to be something you're not, but by embodying love, justice, and welcome right where you are.

Practice Hospitality and Inclusion

This means more than tolerating one another. It's about building the kinds of communities in which your story is honored, your presence is celebrated, and your pain is not ignored. That kind of welcome—the kind Jesus showed—is what we're called to extend, especially to those who've been pushed to the margins.

Challenge Systems That Divide

You already know this truth: Some of the deepest wounds come not from personal prejudice but from systems set up to exclude. If Jesus tore down the dividing wall, then we are called to do the same. That includes speaking up in your church, your workplace, your city—wherever those systems still separate and silence. Don't let anyone tell you the gospel is only about personal salvation. Jesus didn't just save souls—he created a new people through regeneration.

Ephesians 2 doesn't ask you to pretend that the past didn't happen. It doesn't call you to ignore what's still broken. It invites you to stand in the power of what Jesus already did. To know that, in him, your place is secure. Your identity is restored. And your calling is clear.

Because this isn't just about coexisting. It's about *belonging*—to one another, to the body of Christ, and to the God who made us one.

Oneness isn't a polite suggestion.

The fruit of real reconciliation leads to oneness.

And it's part of the story you've been entrusted to live.

NINE

Hope for the Future

YOU'VE WALKED WITH ME THROUGH SOME hard truths. We've named the wounds—how Christianity was distorted, weaponized, and stripped down to serve the powerful. We've traced the lies, the erasures, the systems that claimed God but looked nothing like Jesus. And we've sat with the ache of that legacy, not just in the past, but in our own lives.

But I've also shown you what we can reclaim as ours. You've seen how the gospel took root in African soil long before slave ships crossed the Atlantic. You've heard the voices of those who held on to a Jesus who sets captives free. You've stood with prophets, preachers, and everyday people who refused to let whitewashed theology have the final word. And maybe, as I have, you've started to believe that something deeper really is possible.

I still remember standing in front of the Slave Bible—shocked at what had been removed and stirred by what remained.

They tried to cut out justice. They tried to silence liberation. But the Word of God is living. The very existence of that Bible is proof of the distortion—but also of the resilience. Because the gospel survived. And so did we.

The faith in your Black skin is not borrowed. It's not a footnote. It's a testimony. A testimony that God's Spirit was never confined to the slave quarters, the brush harbors, or the footnotes of Western theology. You are the living continuation of a faith that outlasted chains, outsang the lash, and dared to believe in a God who hears.

Because at the center of this whole journey is a simple, powerful truth: The church Jesus came to build is still possible. A church rooted in his lordship and resurrection power. A church that proclaims salvation and disciples people toward maturity. A church that worships in Spirit and in truth—and, yes, a church that also reflects his justice, grace, and reconciling love.

Not a church built on cultural comfort or respectability. Not one that props up injustice in the name of order. But a Spirit-filled, boundary-breaking, truth-telling, justice-doing, love-soaked community that bears witness to the kingdom of God—on earth as it is in heaven.

That's the vision pulling us forward. That's the kind of church we're called to help build—not in our own strength, but by the power of the Spirit at work in us.

Not in theory.

Not someday.
But right here. Right now.

> Your people will rebuild the ancient ruins
> and will raise up the age-old foundations;
> you will be called Repairer of Broken Walls,
> Restorer of Streets with Dwellings.
>
> —Isaiah 58:12

A Vision of the True Church Is a New Body

The church I see in Scripture—and the one I've caught glimpses of in my own life—isn't built on sameness. It's built on surrender. It's not united by culture, politics, or skin tone. It's united by Christ.

Jesus never prayed that we would be identical. He prayed that we would be one.

That vision still wrecks me. Because I've seen what it looks like when the church gets it right. Not perfectly. Not easily. But faithfully.

I've seen it when people from radically different backgrounds gather not to perform unity but to pursue it—for real. I've seen it in tears at the altar, in prayer circles where nobody's looking for credit, in congregations that dare to talk about race without running from it. That's not theory. That's the Spirit at work.

The true church doesn't minimize difference—it dignifies it. It listens before it speaks. It tells the truth about injustice. It honors the stories we carry—especially the ones the world tries to bury. And then it goes beyond talk. It builds something new.

This kind of church isn't just multiethnic on the surface. It's rooted in love, shaped by repentance, and grounded in justice. It takes seriously the call to bear one another's burdens, to confess and forgive, to stay at the table even when it's hard.

And here's what gives me hope: I've seen that church growing. In my own congregation, which has been historically Black for more than eighty years, I've watched as God has slowly drawn in people of different cultures and ethnicities—not because we chased diversity, but because we pursued Christ. We've never erased our Blackness. We've never stopped preaching justice. But as we've followed Jesus, the Spirit has expanded our circle.

That's what the gospel does. It doesn't flatten us—it frees us. It doesn't erase our stories—it redeems them. The church that Jesus died for isn't an illusion. It's a reality we are called to live into.

Together.

A Glimpse of Hope

I will never forget the day it happened. I had just preached on racism and injustice, naming it plainly, unapologetically, as sin. I ended the message with an altar call. But this one wasn't for salvation in the usual sense. It was for surrender. I invited anyone who had carried racism, prejudice, or bitterness—on either side—to come and lay it at the feet of Jesus.

And then I watched something holy unfold.

Among the many who came forward, I saw a white man walk slowly to the altar. His shoulders were trembling. He dropped to his knees, weeping. Loudly. Visibly. He cried out to God asking for forgiveness—not just for his own bias, but for the system he had been part of. And then, before I could even take it all in, one of our Black church members moved toward him. He didn't stand above him. He knelt down too. Wrapped his arms around him. And began to pray.

In that moment, no one was trying to be impressive. No one was performing. We were just the church—raw, real, surrendered. People from every background, linked arm in arm, letting go of past wounds and letting God do what only he can: make us one.

It wasn't tidy. It wasn't perfect. But it was sacred.

That day, we didn't just preach on reconciliation and oneness. We lived it. And for a moment I saw with my own eyes what Revelation 7:9 points to—a church from every nation, tribe, people, and language worshiping the Lamb together.

We're not there yet. But I hold on to that day as a down payment. A glimpse. A reminder that the Spirit is still moving, still healing, still making all things new.

A Personal Witness

I don't pretend to have all the answers.

Like you, I'm still learning—still working out what it

means to follow Jesus fully in this skin, in this world, with this history. I've spent years preaching, teaching, pastoring, reading and researching, leading and listening. And I still feel the tension. The weight of it all. But I also feel the pull of something deeper—something more beautiful than the division and distortion we've inherited. The call of the gospel that reconciles all things to Christ.

In my own ministry, I've sought to build a church that reflects that calling—a vision of the new body of Christ in which all races and ethnicities are welcomed, seen, and honored with dignity and worth. Our church has deep Black roots. That history isn't just acknowledged—it's cherished. And yet, over time, we've begun to reflect something even broader—Black and brown, white and Asian, native born and immigrant, young and old. I believe that's the fruit of the gospel. Not because we've chased diversity for diversity's sake, but because we've chased Jesus. And when you chase Jesus, you will run into people who don't look like you. You'll find unity, not through erasure, but through grace.

That same intentionality shapes my relationships. My closest friendships, my academic colleagues, my spiritual community—they span cultures, languages, and life experiences. I've found fellowship with white, Asian, and Latino brothers and sisters who not only accept me but also embrace me. I don't have to check my Blackness at the door. In these spaces, our differences are not just tolerated—they're treasured.

This isn't easy work. It's costly. Sometimes lonely. Always

vulnerable. But I stay in it because I believe in the vision of the church that God has given us—a church where justice and truth don't live in tension with love and unity but are braided together by the Spirit. A church that takes seriously the call in Ephesians to destroy the dividing wall of hostility, not with slogans or shallow peace, but through the reconciling blood of Jesus.

And I write these words to you not just as a pastor but as a brother. As someone who's been wounded by the church and healed by it. As someone who knows the pain of exclusion but refuses to give up on the beauty of Christ's body.

You may still be wondering whether this faith is worth holding on to. I get it. But let me leave you with this: There is no other story that dignifies your Blackness, your history, and your hope like the gospel of Jesus Christ. There is no other truth that calls us into something deeper than survival—into transformation. There is no other power that can turn generational pain into generational healing.

The road ahead is long. But you don't walk it alone.

This Faith Has Always Been Yours

The gospel is good news. Still.

Even with the ways it's been manipulated. Even with the chapters soaked in violence and distortion. Even with how it's been used to dehumanize Black people and exalt whiteness as divine.

That wasn't the gospel. That was a lie from the pit of hell.

The gospel has never been about race, color, racism, injustice, or justice.

It's about redemption.

It's about eternity.

It's about a Savior who offers salvation to all humanity through his death and resurrection.

The danger of only seeing the bad news is this: If I let the distortion define my faith, I might miss the real Jesus. I might miss the grace that's been chasing me my whole life.

And I refuse to give anybody that kind of power over my faith.

I refuse to let what they got wrong keep me from what God made right.

The evil they did wasn't of God—it was the devil's work.

And even more? This faith was never theirs to begin with.

Long before slavery, long before European missionaries, my African ancestors walked with God. We've always been in the Book. We've always been part of the story. We've been bishops and theologians, desert fathers and faithful mothers. Our spiritual legacy is older than American Christianity. Older than colonial missions. Older than the slave ships that tried to strip us of it.

So no—I'm not clinging to a white man's religion.

I'm reclaiming a faith that has always been mine.

For years, we've been forced to wrestle with the question *Can I be Black and Christian?*

Because the Christianity handed down to us in this country often made it seem as if we had to choose.

But I'm here to tell you: *No more choosing.*

I am unapologetically Black. And I am unapologetically Christian. And I see no contradiction.

I am unapologetically Black *and* Christian.

I can embrace the gospel and my Black skin!

Because in Christ I am fully seen, fully known, fully loved, and fully called.

This Is Not the End

If you've made it this far, I want to say something simple but true: I see you.

You've carried more than history—you've carried heartache. You've wrestled with hard questions. You've refused to settle for shallow answers. And still, here you are, holding on to Jesus. Not blindly. Not because someone told you to. But because somewhere deep in your spirit you know: He is still good.

And now the question is this: What do we do with that?

We walk forward.

Not in fear. Not in cynicism. But in faith.

We live as if the gospel really is good news for us. We build churches where our children don't have to wonder whether their skin is a curse or their culture a complication. We open our Bibles and see not just the pain of the past but the promise of restoration. We tear down the dividing walls, not just with theology, but with our lives.

You don't have to wait for permission. You don't need to be perfect. You just need to be willing to let God use your voice, your story, your presence in the places he's planted you.

Because this isn't the end of the story. It's the beginning of reclamation.

And we know how the story ends:

> Therefore God exalted him to the highest place
> and gave him the name that is above
> every name,
> that at the name of Jesus every knee
> should bow,
> in heaven and on earth and under the
> earth,
> and every tongue acknowledge that Jesus
> Christ is Lord,
> to the glory of God the Father.
>
> —PHILIPPIANS 2:9–11

That's where we're headed. Every tongue. Every tribe. Every people. Bowing together—not in fear, but in awe. Not in erasure, but in fullness. Not by losing who we are, but by bringing our whole selves into the presence of the one who made us.

Because your Black skin was never a problem for God. It was part of his plan.

Because the gospel was never meant to chain you. It was meant to free you.

Because Jesus isn't done with his church. And he's not done with you.

So let's keep going.

Let's keep building.

Let's give the world a glimpse—just a glimpse—of what heaven will look like when we finally bow, together, and call him Lord.

Notes

INTRODUCTION: WHAT DO WE DO WITH THIS FAITH?

1. Besheer Mohamed et al., "Faith Among Black Americans," Pew Research Center, February 16, 2021, www.pewresearch.org/religion/2021/02/16/faith-among-black-americans.
2. Barna Group, *Where Do We Go from Here? The Future of the Black Church*, 2022.
3. Thomas C. Oden, *How Africa Shaped the Christian Mind: Rediscovering the African Seedbed of Western Christianity* (InterVarsity Press, 2007), 9.
4. Fannie Lou Hamer, "We're On Our Way," in *The Speeches of Fannie Lou Hamer: To Tell It Like It Is*, ed. Maegan Parker Brooks and Davis W. Houck (University Press of Mississippi, 2011), 55.

ONE: WHEN FAITH WAS WEAPONIZED

1. David M. Whitford, *The Curse of Ham: Race and Slavery in Early Judaism, Christianity, and Islam* (Ashgate Publishing, 2009), 36.

2. Whitford, *Curse of Ham*, 19–21.
3. Whitford, *Curse of Ham*.
4. Charles Hodge, "The Bible Argument on Slavery," *Biblical Repertory and Princeton Review* (1851).
5. Whitford, *Curse of Ham*, 304.
6. Josiah Priest, *Bible Defence of Slavery* (J. F. Brennan, 1851), 99, https://archive.org/details/bibledefenceofsl00inprie/page/98/mode/2up.
7. Whitford, *Curse of Ham*, 256–57.
8. Whitford, *Curse of Ham*, 306.
9. Whitford, *Curse of Ham*, 36.
10. Stephen R. Haynes, *Noah's Curse: The Biblical Justification of American Slavery* (Oxford University Press, 2002), 79.
11. Mark A. Noll, *The Civil War as a Theological Crisis* (University of North Carolina Press, 2006), 41–45; Whitford, *Curse of Ham*, 36–38.
12. Eugene D. Genovese, *A Consuming Fire: The Fall of the Confederacy in the Mind of the White Christian South* (University of Georgia Press, 1998), 57.
13. Hodge, "Bible Argument on Slavery"; Whitford, *Curse of Ham*, 88–92.
14. Whitford, *Curse of Ham*, 73–75.

TWO: STILL THE MOST SEGREGATED HOUR

1. Martin Luther King Jr., "Interview on *Meet the Press*," NBC, April 17, 1960. Transcript published by The Martin Luther King, Jr., Research and Education Institute, Stanford University, https://kinginstitute.stanford.edu/king-papers/documents/interview-meet-press.
2. Marissa Postell, "Most Pastors See Racial Diversity in the Church as a Goal but Not Reality," Lifeway Research, February 15, 2022, https://research.lifeway.com/2022/02/15

/most-pastors-see-racial-diversity-in-the-church-as-a-goal-but-not-reality.

3. Michael O. Emerson and Christian Smith, *Divided by Faith: Evangelical Religion and the Problem of Race in America* (Oxford University Press, 2000). In chapter 3, Emerson and Smith discuss biblical justifications for segregation, including the use of Acts 17:26.
4. Bob Jones Sr., *Is Segregation Scriptural?* (Bob Jones University Press, 1960), 19.
5. R. J. Reinhart, "Protests Seen as Harming Civil Rights Movement in '60s," Gallup Vault, January 21, 2019, https://news.gallup.com/vault/246167/protests-seen-harming-civil-rights-movement-60s.aspx.
6. Justin Taylor, "A Conversation with Four Historians on the Response of White Evangelicals to the Civil Rights Movement," The Gospel Coalition, July 1, 2016, www.thegospelcoalition.org/blogs/evangelical-history/a-conversation-with-four-historians-on-the-response-of-white-evangelicals-to-the-civil-rights-movement.
7. Martin Luther King Jr., "Letter from Birmingham Jail," April 16, 1963, African Studies Center, University of Pennsylvania, accessed August 22, 2025, www.africa.upenn.edu/Articles_Gen/Letter_Birmingham.html.
8. Emerson and Smith, *Divided by Faith*, 72–73.
9. Edward J. Blum and Paul Harvey, *The Color of Christ: The Son of God and the Saga of Race in America* (University of North Carolina Press, 2012), 148–50.
10. Stephen R. Haynes, "Distinction and Dispersal: Folk Theology and the Maintenance of White Supremacy," *Journal of Southern Religion* 17 (2015), https://jsreligion.org/issues/vol17/haynes.html.
11. Neil R. McMillen, *The Citizens' Council: Organized*

Resistance to the Second Reconstruction, 1954–64 (University of Illinois Press, 1994), 138.

12. James H. Cone, *The Cross and the Lynching Tree* (Orbis Books, 2011), 81.
13. Richard Allen, *The Life, Experience, and Gospel Labors of the Rt. Rev. Richard Allen* (Philadelphia, 1880), 23.
14. Equal Justice Initiative, "Interracial Group Arrested for Entering Segregated Mississippi Churches," *A History of Racial Injustice Calendar*, March 29, 1964, https://calendar.eji.org/racial-injustice/mar/29.
15. Sam Hodges, "Mississippi Pastors Paid Price for Segregation Challenge," United Methodist News Service, January 14, 2013. https://www.umnews.org/en/news/mississippi-pastors-paid-price-for-segregation-challenge.
16. "A History of Private Schools and Race in the American South," Southern Education Foundation, originally published in 2016, accessed August 22, 2025, https://southerneducation.org/publications/history-of-private-schools-and-race-in-the-american-south.
17. Kevin M. Kruse, *White Flight: Atlanta and the Making of Modern Conservatism* (Princeton University Press, 2005). For a discussion on the role of White Citizens' Councils and their religious framing, see Johnny E. Williams, *Decoding Racial Ideology in Genomics* (Lexington Books, 2016).
18. Jemar Tisby, *The Color of Compromise: The Truth About the American Church's Complicity in Racism* (Zondervan, 2019), 7.
19. King, "Letter from Birmingham Jail."
20. Juan Williams, *Eyes on the Prize: America's Civil Rights Years, 1954–1965* (Penguin, 1988), 231–33.
21. David L. Chappell, *A Stone of Hope: Prophetic Religion and the Death of Jim Crow* (University of North Carolina Press, 2004), 167–70.

22. Charles Marsh, *God's Long Summer: Stories of Faith and Civil Rights* (Princeton University Press, 1997), 38–40.
23. "New Black Church Is Firebombed in All-White Providence, Rhode Island, Neighborhood," Equal Justice Initiative, History of Racial Injustice Daily Calendar, August 15, https://calendar.eji.org/racial-injustice/aug/15.
24. "New Black Church Is Firebombed."
25. Max Blau, "Church Burnings after Charleston: Part of a 'Long, Dark' History That Never Stopped," *The Guardian*, July 2, 2015, www.theguardian.com/us-news/2015/jul/02/us-church-burnings-race-south-carolina.
26. Debbie Elliott, "Lessons from Birmingham: 60 Years After the 16th Street Baptist Church Bombing," NPR, September 14, 2023, www.npr.org/2023/09/14/1199312953/16th-street-baptist-church-bombing-60th-anniversary.
27. *Church Arson Prevention Act of 1996: Hearing Before the Subcommittee on Crime*, 104th Cong., 2nd Sess. (June 19, 1996).
28. Isabel Wilkerson, *The Warmth of Other Suns: The Epic Story of America's Great Migration* (Random House, 2010), 9.
29. Richard Rothstein, *The Color of Law: A Forgotten History of How Our Government Segregated America* (Liveright Publishing, 2017).
30. Beryl Satter, *Family Properties: Race, Real Estate, and the Exploitation of Black Urban America* (Metropolitan Books, 2009).
31. *Report on the Economic Well-Being of U.S. Households in 2017* (Federal Reserve Board, May 2018), www.federalreserve.gov/publications/files/2017-report-economic-well-being-us-households-201805.pdf.
32. Jill Sheridan, "A Black Woman Says She Had to Hide Her Race to Get a Fair Home Appraisal," NPR, May 21, 2021,

www.npr.org/2021/05/21/998536881/a-black-woman -says-she-had-to-hide-her-race-to-get-a-fair-home-appraisal.

33. Vanessa Romo, "Black Couple Settles Lawsuit Claiming Their Home Appraisal Was Lowballed Due to Bias," NPR, updated March 9, 2023, www.npr.org/2023/03/09 /1162103286/home-appraisal-racial-bias-black-homeowners -lawsuit.
34. Romo, "Black Couple Settles Lawsuit."
35. "Racial and Ethnic Valuation Gaps in Home Purchase Appraisals," Freddie Mac, September 2021, https://web .archive.org/web/20220316005532/https://www.freddiemac .com/research/insight/20210920-home-appraisals.
36. Andre Perry et al., "The Devaluation of Assets in Black Neighborhoods: The Case of Residential Property," Brookings Institution, November 27, 2018, www.brookings .edu/research/devaluation-of-assets-in-black-neighborhoods.
37. Michelle Alexander, *The New Jim Crow: Mass Incarceration in the Age of Colorblindness*, rev. ed. (New Press, 2012), 2.
38. Dan Baum, "Legalize It All: How to Win the War on Drugs," *Harper's Magazine*, April 2016, https://harpers.org/archive /2016/04/legalize-it-all.
39. *Report to the Congress: Cocaine and Federal Sentencing Policy* (United States Sentencing Commission, May 2007), www.ussc.gov/sites/default/files/pdf/news/congressional -testimony-and-reports/drug-topics/200705_RtC_Cocaine _Sentencing_Policy.pdf.
40. Ashley Nellis, "Mass Incarceration Trends," The Sentencing Project, May 2024, 5, www.sentencingproject.org/app /uploads/2024/05/Mass-Incarceration-Trends.pdf.
41. Nellis, "Mass Incarceration Trends," 6.
42. *Prevalence of Imprisonment in the U.S. Population, 1974–2001* (US Department of Justice, Bureau of Justice Statistics,

August 2003), https://bjs.ojp.gov/library/publications/prevalence-imprisonment-us-population-1974-2001.

43. Aaron Griffith, *God's Law and Order: The Politics of Punishment in Evangelical America* (Harvard University Press, 2020), 15.
44. Griffith, *God's Law and Order*, 21.
45. Lea Hunter, "What You Need to Know About Ending Cash Bail," Center for American Progress, last updated April 23, 2020, www.americanprogress.org/article/ending-cash-bail.
46. *Revoked: How Probation and Parole Feed Mass Incarceration in the United States* (Human Rights Watch and ACLU, 2020), www.hrw.org/sites/default/files/media_2020/07/us_supervision0720_web_1.pdf.
47. *Report to the United Nations on Racial Disparities in the U.S. Criminal Justice System* (Sentencing Project, April 19, 2018), www.sentencingproject.org/publications/un-report-on-racial-disparities.
48. Andrew L. Whitehead and Samuel L. Perry, *Taking America Back for God: Christian Nationalism in the United States* (Oxford: Oxford University Press, 2020).
49. "Do Multiracial Churches Offer Healthy Community for Non-White Attendees?" Barna Group, April 28, 2021, www.barna.com/research/multiracial-church.
50. Kate Shellnutt, "Black Millennials and Gen Z Becoming More Cynical Toward Christian Identity," *Christianity Today*, April 15, 2021, www.christianitytoday.com/news/2021/april/black-gen-z-millennial-christian-church-trends-barna.html.

THREE: BLACK AMERICANS ARE LEAVING CHURCH

1. Albert J. Raboteau, *Slave Religion: The "Invisible Institution" in the Antebellum South* (Oxford University Press, 2004), 290.

2. Lisa Fields, "Listening and Loving Those with Questions: An Interview with Lisa Fields," Redeemer City to City, November 18, 2021, https://redeemercitytocity.com /articles-stories/lisa-fields-interview.
3. Ryan P. Burge, "Black Americans See the Biggest Shift Away from Faith," *Christianity Today*, February 15, 2022, www .christianitytoday.com/news/2022/february/black-american -nones-faith-unaffiliation-nothing.html.
4. Willie James Jennings, *The Christian Imagination: Theology and the Origins of Race* (Yale University Press, 2010), 6.
5. Martin Luther King Jr., "Letter from Birmingham Jail," April 16, 1963, African Studies Center, University of Pennsylvania, accessed August 22, 2025, www.africa.upenn .edu/Articles_Gen/Letter_Birmingham.html.
6. Anthea Butler, *White Evangelical Racism: The Politics of Morality in America* (University of North Carolina Press, 2021).
7. *A Christian Nation? Understanding the Threat of Christian Nationalism to American Democracy and Culture*, Public Religion Research Institute and Brookings Institution, February 2023, https://prri.org/wp-content/uploads /2025/05/PRRI-Jan-2023-Christian-Nationalism-Final-1.pdf.
8. Yonat Shimron, "Poll: A Third of Americans Are Christian Nationalists and Most Are White Evangelicals," Religion News Service, February 8, 2023, https://religionnews.com /2023/02/08/a-third-of-americans-are-christian-nationalists -and-most-are-white-evangelicals.

FOUR: RECLAIMING CHRISTIANITY'S AFRICAN ROOTS

1. Thomas C. Oden, *How Africa Shaped the Christian Mind: Rediscovering the African Seedbed of Western Christianity* (IVP Academic, 2007), 19.
2. Kwame Bediako, *Christianity in Africa: The Renewal of a*

Non-Western Religion (Edinburgh University Press, 1995), 24–36.

3. John Binns, *The Orthodox Church of Ethiopia: A History* (I. B. Tauris, 2016), 5–10.
4. Cyprian of Carthage, *On the Unity of the Church*, in *The Ante-Nicene Fathers*, vol. 5: *Fathers of the Third Century: Hippolytus, Cyprian, Caius, Novatian, Appendix*, ed. Alexander Roberts and James Donaldson (Christian Literature Publishing Co., 1886), 423.

FIVE: FAITH-FUELED RESISTANCE

1. Nat Turner, *The Confessions of Nat Turner* (Baltimore, 1831), Project Gutenberg, www.gutenberg.org/cache/epub/15333/pg15333-images.html.
2. Turner, *Confessions.*
3. Turner, *Confessions.*
4. Vincent Harding, *There Is a River: The Black Struggle for Freedom in America* (Harcourt Brace Jovanovich, 1981), 79.
5. Douglas Brinkley, *Rosa Parks: A Life* (Penguin Books, 2000), 211.
6. Martin Luther King Jr., "I Have a Dream," speech delivered at Washington, DC, August 28, 1963, NPR, updated January 16, 2023, www.npr.org/2010/01/18/122701268/i-have-a-dream-speech-in-its-entirety.
7. Martin Luther King Jr., "Letter from Birmingham Jail," April 16, 1963, African Studies Center, University of Pennsylvania, accessed August 22, 2025, www.africa.upenn.edu/Articles_Gen/Letter_Birmingham.html.
8. Martin Luther King Jr., *Stride Toward Freedom: The Montgomery Story* (Harper & Row, 1958), 85.
9. Howard Thurman, *Jesus and the Disinherited* (Beacon Press, 1976), 15–16.

10. James H. Cone, *Black Theology and Black Power* (Orbis Books, 2021), 5–8.
11. Randal Maurice Jelks, *Benjamin Elijah Mays, Schoolmaster of the Movement: A Biography* (University of North Carolina Press, 2012), 242.
12. John Lewis, "Speech at the March on Washington for Jobs and Freedom," August 28, 1963. See "John Lewis' Historic Speech at the March on Washington," NowThis Impact, YouTube, July 28, 2020, 4:12, www.youtube.com/watch?v=TCqR9LbT1_w.
13. "Who Was Ella Baker," Ella Baker Center for Human Rights, accessed August 26, 2025, https://ellabakercenter.org/who-was-ella-baker.
14. James H. Cone, *God of the Oppressed*, rev. ed. (Orbis Books, 1997), 151.

SIX: THE GOD BEHIND THE RESISTANCE

1. Bruce K. Waltke, *The Book of Proverbs, Chapters 1–15* (Eerdmans, 2004), 97.
2. Eric Mason, *Woke Church: An Urgent Call for Christians in America to Confront Racism and Injustice* (Moody, 2018), 75.
3. Nicholas Wolterstorff, *Justice: Rights and Wrongs* (Princeton University Press, 2008), 373.
4. Eddie Byun, *Justice Awakening: How You and Your Church Can Help End Human Trafficking* (IVP, 2014), 78.

SEVEN: EVERY PERSON IS MADE IN THE IMAGE OF GOD

1. Millard J. Erickson, *Introducing Christian Doctrine* (Baker Academic, 2001), 177.
2. Wayne Grudem, *Systematic Theology: An Introduction to Biblical Doctrine* (Zondervan, 1994), 443.
3. Grudem, *Systematic Theology*, 450.

4. US Const. art. I, § 2, National Archives, www.archives.gov/founding-docs/constitution-transcript.
5. Akhil Reed Amar, *America's Constitution: A Biography* (Random House, 2005), 89.
6. Frederick Douglass, "What to the Slave Is the Fourth of July?," speech delivered at Rochester, New York, July 5, 1852, in *The Life and Writings of Frederick Douglass*, vol. 2, ed. Philip S. Foner (New York: International Publishers, 1950), 192.
7. Howard Thurman, *Jesus and the Disinherited* (Beacon Press, 1976), 94.
8. Martin Luther King Jr., "Facing the Challenge of a New Age," address delivered at the First Annual Institute on Nonviolence and Social Change, December 3, 1956, in *A Testament of Hope: The Essential Writings and Speeches of Martin Luther King Jr.*, ed. James M. Washington (HarperCollins, 1986), 138.
9. Daniel Alexander Payne, "Address to the Educational Convention," 1839, in Carol V. R. George, *Segregated Sabbaths: Richard Allen and the Emergence of Independent Black Churches 1760–1840* (New York: Oxford University Press, 1973), 153.
10. James H. Cone, *A Black Theology of Liberation* (Lippincott, 1970), 118.

EIGHT: ONENESS

1. Clinton Arnold, *Zondervan Illustrated Bible Backgrounds Commentary*, vol. 3: *Romans to Philemon*, (Zondervan, 2002, 317.
2. Arnold, *Romans to Philemon*, 317.
3. Clinton E. Arnold, *Ephesians*, Zondervan Exegetical Commentary on the New Testament, ed. Clinton E. Arnold (Zondervan, 2010), 164–65.

4. Miroslav Volf, *Exclusion and Embrace: A Theological Exploration of Identity, Otherness, and Reconciliation* (Abingdon, 1996), 44.
5. John Stott, *God's New Society: The Message of Ephesians* (IVP, 1979), 107.
6. Brenda Salter McNeil, *Roadmap to Reconciliation 2.0: Moving Communities into Unity, Wholeness, and Justice* (IVP, 2020), 15.